Sept

To Maxine

A Wonderful friend
to dragons,

Dragon Talks
Puppet Scripts for Lectionary Year C

Peace

Robbie

AKA

J. Lippard

dragon talks

Puppet Scripts for Lectionary Year C

James Lepard

Editor: Michael Schwartzentruber
Cover design: Cyrus Gandevia
Interior and pre-press production: Cyrus Gandevia
Cover image: © Teguh Mujiono
Proofreader: Dianne Greenslade

GOLD
BNC CERTIFIED | BIBLIOGRAPHIC DATA 2014-15

Wood Lake is an imprint of Wood Lake Publishing, Inc. Wood Lake Publishing acknowledges the financial support of the Government of Canada, through the Canada Book Fund (CBF) for its publishing activities. Wood Lake Publishing also acknowledges the financial support of the Province of British Columbia through the Book Publishing Tax Credit.

At Wood Lake Publishing, we practise what we publish, being guided by a concern for fairness, justice, and equal opportunity in all of our relationships with employees and customers. Wood Lake Publishing is committed to caring for the environment and all creation. Wood Lake Publishing recycles, reuses, and encourages readers to do the same. Resources are printed on 100% post-consumer recycled paper and more environmentally friendly groundwood papers (newsprint), whenever possible. A percentage of all profit is donated to charitable organizations.

Library and Archives Canada Cataloguing in Publication

Lepard, James, 1965-, author
    Dragon talks : puppet scripts for lectionary year C
/ James Lepard.

Issued in print and electronic formats.
ISBN 978-1-77064-794-7 (pbk.).--ISBN 978-1-77064-797-8
(html)

    1. Puppet plays, Canadian (English). 2. Bible plays, Canadian
(English). I. Title.

PS8623.E633D73 2015   C812'.6   C2015-902972-4
                                     C2015-902973-2

Published by Wood Lake
An imprint of Wood Lake Publishing Inc.
485 Beaver Lake Road, Kelowna, BC, Canada, V4V 1S5
www.woodlake.com
1.800.663.2775
Printing 10 9 8 7 6 5 4 3 2 1
Printed in Canada

Dedication

To Marcus Borg
(March 11, 1942–January 21, 2015)
my teacher and companion on the Christian journey

"It may not have happened this way, but I know it's true." – Black Elk:
As quoted in Marcus Borg, *Convictions: How I learned what matters most*

Acknowledgements

All those who have or will be friends to dragons!

CONTENTS

INTRODUCTION

What You Need to Know about Your Dragon...Talks

The "Robbie" project began over 15 years ago when, during a weekly staff meeting, my ministry partner presented a resource for children's time by Peter J. Mead called *"God talks" with Gabby*. Included in the resource were a hand puppet and a series of scripts that followed the lectionary readings for Year A. The scripts were designed as a conversation between the puppet and the pastor.

Over the year, we introduced the puppet *Gabby* to the congregation and discovered that the scripted conversation format was very well-received and that people waited each week to hear what Gabby had to say.

Subsequently, I began to write my own scripts, scripts that reflected my own theological and imaginative take on the lectionary texts, as well as our unique congregational context.

One day my ministry partner introduced me to a large dragon puppet and suggested that we use this puppet for our children's time.

Sitting in my partner's office, she asked me, "What will you call him?" I looked at the big googly-eyed puppet and said, "Robbie." I soon discovered that when Robbie spoke he was decidedly a Celtic puppet, with a voice that was a cross between the groundskeeper Willie from *The Simpsons*, the father in Mike Meyer's *I Married an Axe Murderer*, and Father Dougal of BBC's *Father Ted* series. Thus Robbie the Dragon was born, and he has been part of the ministry with the two congregations I've served for the past 15 years.

Just like in the first *Harry Potter* book, where Harry discovers that "the wand chooses the wizard," so too will each puppet have its own voice, as the puppeteer will discover through play and experimentation. In terms of voice, while Robbie was decidedly Celtic, not all puppets need to have an accent and, in fact, probably *shouldn't* have an accent given that accents can be an effect that stereotypes a group of people in a disparaging way. I have voiced other puppets and in finding a voice for the character, I play with pitch, timbre, and pace of speech until a voice suited to the character emerges.

A dragon may seem an odd choice for a church puppet. A dragon has often been portrayed as figure of danger, evil, destruction, and violence. Perhaps the most famous dragon in church history is the dragon in the legend of St. George and the Dragon. This legend has its historical origins during the time of the crusades, a time during which the West sought to dominate and assimilate the East and its people under the imperial rule of "Christendom." The means of such assimilation was through coercion, threats of violence, and actual systematic violence. In today's popular culture, the dragon continues to represent the "other."

In the movie *How to Train Your Dragon*, dragons represent destruction, violence, and evil, until one young boy befriends a dragon and comes to recognize that such descriptions are the products of fear, ignorance, and misunderstanding.

Stieg Larsson's *The Girl with the Dragon Tattoo* series of novels uses the image of the dragon not only as a symbol of power, but Lisbeth Salander's dragon tattoo becomes a metaphoric symbol of strength and courage for the heroine, who is often feared because of her appearance and her unconventional behaviour.

Perhaps the dragon represents our conscious and unconscious fear and distrust of the "other." Within the Christian community and within ourselves we still have our "dragons" – anyone whose ideas or personality we perceive as a threat to our communities or to ourselves. Christian communities often perceive those of different faiths as dragons, those of different sexual orientation as dragons, those whose ethnicity is not of the dominant culture within the community, those who are disabled with mental or physical disabilities, those whose appearance does not mesh with the status quo. We often fear these people, and our response to what we fear is to either destroy or dominate, which is antithetical to the Way of Jesus, who embraced and often saw in the outsider a person more fully representing the vision of God's Kindom.

In his book *Why Did Jesus, Moses, the Buddha, and Mohammed Cross the Road?: Christian Identity in a Multi-Faith World*, Brian McLaren writes,

Whether we realize it or not most of us who suffer from CRIS (Conflicted Religious Identity Syndrome) are trying to distance ourselves from religious hostility. I mean opposition, the sense that the other is the enemy. Hostility makes one unwilling to be a host (the two words are historically related). The other must be turned away, kept at a distance as unwanted outsider, not welcomed in hospitality as a guest or friend (p.19).

Introducing Robbie the Dragon to the congregation was an invitation, and an ongoing process of learning, to continually challenge our primordial exclusivity. It was an invitation and challenge to open ourselves to be a community that practises asking questions; living compassion; seeking to know one another and the "other"; and growing in faith, hope, justice, and love for all of God's creations.

From a practical point of view, for anyone who has to do it on a regular basis, the task of "doing" the children's time each week can be more nerve wracking than creating a sermon each week. I have been in congregations with large numbers of children, as well as in congregations with only one or two children. Each situation brings familiar challenges. For example, you never know how many children will be present on any given Sunday. How are you going to deal with the precocious child who sees children's time as an opportunity to take the stage, grab the microphone, and unwittingly sabotage the experience? It is often a challenge to make children's time an engaging, meaningful experience – one that doesn't simply exploit both the minister and the children.

As a result, I question the traditional children's time format of "would the children like to come to the front now?" On one level, the format may appear to be interactive and engaging; however, my experience has been that this format can be an awkward time for all. First, not all of the children are keen to be on display for the congregation, and it often feels like a set-up for both the kids and the person leading children's time. Often the congregation is primed to laugh not *with* the kids, but *at* the kids, and the person leading the children's time is often on the spot for crowd control. As a result, the supposed "conversation" has an expected agenda and right answer, which is usually "God," "Jesus," or "love" – all good answers – and kids learn the correct answer without even being asked the question.

Children's time with the puppet conversation eliminates many of the issues associated with children's time.

An advantage of the Robbie conversation is that it works on a level that is accessible for *all ages*. The children and adults look forward to the opportunity to call Robbie from his castle with the weekly "1, 2, 3... *Robbie!*" The introduction itself sets up a sense of expectation; and children's time, though scripted, is participatory – *everyone* is interested and engaged in what Robbie's take on the gospel is this week. On weeks when there is only a small number of children (or none), Robbie still becomes a means by which to engage the text in a fun, open, and irreverent (in the best sense of the word) way. Robbie can ask questions of the text and point out confusing parts in a way that sophisticated church people are afraid to do. As such, the Robbie conversation is a meaningful way to engage the text in an open-ended and playful way. Over the years, many people have commented on how grateful they are for Robbie, because Robbie helped them to appreciate, relate to, and get inside the text.

Recently, a young adult, who was a child when I was the minister in her church, attended a service at the congregation where I now serve. After the service, she approached me. The young woman's face lit up with joy as she talked about Robbie and how much she loved him as a child. I was surprised at her spontaneous and joy-filled response, and it caused me to reflect on the idea that perhaps there is more going on during "Robbie time" than I was aware of.

As a preacher, I will often begin sermon preparation by writing the Robbie script. The process of writing is very much like beginning a conversation with a friend: a friend who does not have a predetermined understanding or agenda of where the conversation is going. It is a conversation that can be playful, thoughtful, and unafraid to go in a variety of directions. Through Robbie, we are given permission to, as St. Paul said, "be fools for Christ," in the hope that what is often seen as foolish in the eyes of the world is *holy* in God's kindom.

Using the Scripts within Worship

Setting the scene
In the congregations I served, we constructed a cardboard screen, which we painted to look like the wall of a castle. There should be an opening, or window, through which Robbie appears.

The "Robbie" puppet
I use a large dragon puppet with a long tail that hangs out over the window (opening) when Robbie appears. However, you can use any size or style of dragon puppet that appeals to you. A Google search for "dragon puppets" will yield a variety of options in a wide price range, or you can make your own.

Suggestions within the scripts
Directions, or suggestions, for how certain lines should be read or acted are included within the scripts, in parentheses.

Placement within the liturgy
A word about the placement of the children's time in the context of the worship service: I typically include Robbie in the liturgy under the heading "We listen for God's Word." First, the scripture is read with the response, "Hear what the Spirit is saying to the church, praise be to you, O Christ."

Readers or "players"
At that point, a member of the congregation moves to the microphone next to Robbie's castle and invites Robbie to come out and share a conversation about the day's lesson. The person speaking with Robbie *varies from week to week*. In the scripts that follow, this person is simply identified as "(Name)." It has been my practice to try to include a wide range of voices representing the congregation: adults, children who can read the script, and sometimes even younger children who can't necessarily read, but who join a parent and are simply happy to be included in the conversation. It is a wonderful testimony to have all ages and stages involved in the engaging process of wrestling with the biblical text.

The disk and sharing the scripts
During the week prior to worship, I will email someone in the congregation and ask if they would like to be Robbie's friend for the upcoming Sunday. In the email, I will include the week's script having substituted their real name for "Name" in the script. The disk that accompanies this book contains a copy of each script as a Word document. This will make it easy for you to revise each script as necessary and to email it to your reader each week. NOTE: Please honour copyright restrictions and refrain from sending these scripts to people who will not be using them within the context of worship within your own congregation.

Hearing the biblical texts
Following the conversation with Robbie, the Word is shared once again through the preached message or sermon. In this way, the Word is heard three times: first in the scripture reading itself, second through the conversation with Robbie, and third through the sermon. Please note that the portion of the biblical text that is included at the beginning of each week's script is *not* read as part of the dialogue; it is included in the script simply to highlight the part of the biblical text that will be the focus of the conversation.

The cumulative effect of this practice is that people are presented with the opportunity to experience and engage with the Word three times (how Trinitarian!) in three unique ways.

Adapt, adapt, adapt

I have written and designed *Dragon Talks* in the hope that these scripts will become part of your ongoing conversation with the Word. I therefore encourage you to alter the scripts in this resource to suit your own contextual and congregational needs. In fact, I hope you will consider writing your own scripts! The theology presented in these scripts is indicative of my own theological perspective and musings. The scripts are therefore not meant to be definitive; rather, they reflect my own ongoing conversation and relationship with the Word. I hope that you find these scripts playful, fun, and engaging, and that they serve to enliven your own ministerial practice.

Advent 1

Luke 21:25–36

21:25 There will be signs in the sun, the moon, and the stars, and on the earth distress among nations confused by the roaring of the sea and the waves.

21:26 People will faint from fear and foreboding of what is coming upon the world, for the powers of the heavens will be shaken.

Name: Good morning everyone, it's great to be here this morning. I sure felt the change in temperature this week. I hope Robbie is getting out his woolies; I know his castle can get pretty chilly sometimes! Let's call him out and see what's up. 1, 2, 3, *Robbie!*

Robbie: I don't know?

Name: Don't know what, Robbie?

Robbie: I didn't know whether or not to come out of my castle this morning.

Name: Why's that, Robbie?

Robbie: Well, the gospel lesson this morning.

Name: Oh, I think I understand. The gospel reading, which talked about the temple being turned upside down.

Robbie: More like blown up!

Name: And wars, and earthquakes…

Robbie: Famines and plagues…

Name: Getting arrested and thrown in jail.

Robbie: Why can't we just sing *Jingle Bells*? Or watch the Santa Claus parade?

Name: Well, Robbie, we can certainly do those things. But Jesus was telling his friends that sometimes life would be uncertain and difficult.

Robbie: Boy, he sure did.

Name: Jesus didn't want to tell his friends that everything in life would be easy. He said there will be times when bad things happen.

Robbie: Well I don't know about you, but now I'm pretty freaked out!

Name: I understand that, Robbie, but Jesus also told his friends to be prepared for when bad things happen.

Robbie: Okay, well let's make sure we've got extra insurance on the castle!

Name: Well…

Robbie: And let's make sure we've got lots of bottled water in the basement…

Name: Well…

Robbie: And canned goods, let's make sure we've got lots canned goods, especially Alpha-Getti. I love Alpha-Getti.

Name: Well…

Robbie: And candles, we've got to stock up on candles, or even better a generator…

Name: Robbie!

Robbie: What?

Name: You're getting yourself all worked up!

Robbie: Well *ya!* Didn't you hear what Jesus said?

Name: I did, Robbie, and I heard Jesus also remind us not to be terrified when we hear rumours that these things are going to happen.

Robbie: But…

Name: But prepare ourselves for when we face difficult situations.

Robbie: Like the generator, the insurance, the candles, and the canned goods…

Name: Robbie, Jesus was also telling us to prepare our hearts and our minds for difficult times.

Robbie: Well, how do we do that?

Name: Remember when Jesus taught us to love one another, to forgive each other?

Robbie: Uh huh.

Name: Remember Jesus' teaching us to care for one another, those who are close to us and even strangers?

Robbie: Uh huh.

Name: Well, Robbie, when we do these things, we prepare ourselves, so when difficult times happen we're not alone.

Robbie: Oh, it's like the time when my castle fell down and friends let me stay at their house.

Name: That's right, Robbie. People's hearts and minds were prepared to help you.

Robbie: I was sure grateful!

Name: That's right, Robbie. You know this week there was a terrible hurricane in the Philippines. People died and many people are without food, or water, or shelter, and we are helping.

Robbie: How are we helping? The Philippines are a long, long way away.

Name: That's true, Robbie, but our congregation, (insert church name), and lots of other congregations in our denomination and in other denominations too, are providing aid to those people.

Robbie: So our hearts and minds were prepared to care for others in difficulty.

Name: That's right, Robbie, so there is no need to worry. If we all prepare our hearts and minds to love and care for one another, we can handle just about anything!

Name: Robbie, where are you going?

Robbie: I've got to call and cancel that generator!

Name: It's good thing we're all called to be generators of care for one another. Amen.

Advent 2

Luke 3:1–6

3:3 He went into all the region around the Jordan, proclaiming a baptism of repentance for the forgiveness of sins

3:4 as it is written in the book of the words of the prophet Isaiah, "The voice of one crying out in the wilderness: 'Prepare the way of the Lord, make his paths straight…'"

Name: Good morning, everyone! It's great to be here on the second Sunday of Advent. I wonder if Robbie can join us and talk about today's lesson. Let's call him out. 1, 2, 3…*Robbie!*… Robbie, are you in there? ROBBIE! (Name knocks on castle)

Robbie: (comes out with ear muffs on his head) Hello, (Name). Sorry, I couldn't hear you.

Name: That's all right, Robbie. How are you?

Robbie: What?

Name: I said…

Robbie: Sorry, I can't hear you!

Name: Maybe it's because you've got earmuffs on your head.

Robbie: No, I don't have any muffins.

Name: (removes ear muffs from Robbie's head) Can you hear me now?

Robbie: Geez, (Name), you don't have to shout. I'm not deaf!

Name: Okay, now that you can hear me, why are you wearing earmuffs?

Robbie: Don't you know which church season we're in?

Name: Well yes, Robbie, this is the second Sunday of Advent!

Robbie: Exactly! It's *Ad vent*. It's the noisiest season of the year.

Name: Robbie, what do you mean?

Robbie: Haven't you noticed at this time of year everywhere you go there are ads to buy this or buy that, the commercials are really loud, and they go on and on and on!

Name: Yes, Robbie, I have noticed that.

Robbie: Well, in my house, every time all the commercials come on TV my mom gets so angry that she starts yelling at the television or computer! She gets so upset she vents her anger by yelling at the commercials. So that's why the four weeks before Christmas become *Ad Vent!*

Name: Oh *now* I understand, Robbie. Your mom's like a lot of people who get frustrated that the weeks before Christmas become all about buying stuff instead of about remembering that *Advent is about preparing* for the Christ to come into our hearts and minds.

Robbie: Exactly!

Name: You know, Robbie, your mom reminds me of John the Baptist in the gospel lesson for this morning.

Robbie: Okay, my mom doesn't always look like she stepped out of *Vogue*, but she's certainly not as wild-looking as John!

Name: No, Robbie. In the gospel lesson this morning, John feels like he's crying in the desert and nobody is listening to him. John's reminding people that the most precious things in life are not stuff, or money, or power, or what clothes you wear and all the things that the ads try to get us to buy.

Robbie: John's telling the people to turn their hearts and minds towards good things.

Name: Godly things.

Robbie: Like when we light the candles on the Advent wreath. The first week we turn our hearts and minds to hope.

Name: And this week we turn our hearts and minds to joy!

Robbie: I love joy! And next week we will light the candle for peace. I can't wait for that candle. Maybe we'll get some peace and Mom will stop yelling at the TV and the ads will stop!

Name: And on the last Sunday before Christmas we light the candle of love!

Robbie: I *love* love! It's the best part of Advent, preparing for God's love. Just like when the world prepared for God's love to come into the world that first Christmas!

Name: Amen.

Robbie: Amen.

Advent 3

Luke 3:7–18

3:7 John said to the crowds that came out to be baptized by him, "You brood of vipers! Who warned you to flee from the wrath to come?

3:8 Bear fruits worthy of repentance...

Name: Good morning, everyone! Well it certainly is getting close to Christmas. I know Robbie is getting very excited! Let's call him out on the count of three. 1, 2, 3...*Robbie!*

Robbie: Is it safe?

Name: What do you mean is it safe?

Robbie: I'm worried.

Name: What are you worried about?

Robbie: The gospel lesson this morning.

Name: Robbie, why has the gospel lesson got you worried?

Robbie: I'm afraid.

Name: Afraid of what?

Robbie: Snakes! In the gospel lesson today, John calls some of the people who came to be baptized *a brood of vipers*! I'm afraid that if I come out of the castle I'll be surrounded by snakes!

Name: Oh, Robbie, I understand. This morning we heard about people coming to John to be baptized.

Robbie: John was offering baptism as a sign that people were willing to turn their lives around and follow God's way.

Name: That's right.

Robbie: So why did he call them a brood of vipers?

Name: Well, Robbie, in the big group of people there were some people who didn't understand what John's baptism meant. It wasn't just about getting wet; it was about changing your ways and committing to a new life.

Robbie: A new life?

Name: That's right: a life of giving to others.

Robbie: Like if I have two pairs of mittens and someone has none...

Name: You share your mittens!

Name: And if I have two cookies in my lunch and someone has none…

Robbie: You share your cookies.

Name: If someone is being bullied, instead of ignoring that person…

Robbie: I could be their friend and say something I like about that person.

Name: The bully and the bullied. Treating others the way you would like to be treated.

Robbie: I get it; John was asking people to try to be loving and caring.

Name: Caring and sharing.

Robbie: Not just at church…

Name: Not just at home, but with everyone.

Robbie: Even with snakes?

Name: Yes, Robbie, even with snakes!

Robbie: Oh boy, I'll have to work on that.

Name: We *all* have to work at being God's people. Amen.

Robbie: Amen.

Advent 4

Luke 1:39–55

1:41 When Elizabeth heard Mary's greeting, the child leaped in her womb. And Elizabeth was filled with the Holy Spirit

1:42 and exclaimed with a loud cry, "Blessed are you among women, and blessed is the fruit of your womb."

Name: Good morning, everyone! Wow, I can't believe it's the last Sunday before Christmas! I'm so excited and I'm sure Robbie is too. Let's call him out and have a chat about this week's lesson! 1, 2, 3… *Robbie!*

Name: Good morning, Robbie.

Robbie: Boxers or briefs?

Name: Robbie, what are you talking about?

Robbie: The gospel lesson, of course. And to be honest with you, (Name), I was quite surprised to hear about underwear in the Bible.

Name: Underwear?

Robbie: Yes! In the gospel lesson this morning it says, "When Elizabeth, Mary's cousin, found out Mary was going to have a baby, she was filled with the Holy Spirit."

Name: I'm with you so far, Robbie, but I still don't know what Mary having a baby has to do with underwear.

Robbie: Well, when she found out Mary was going to have a baby. Elizabeth said, "Mary, blessed are you among women and blessed is the fruit of your *loom!*"

Name: Uh, I don't think she said, "fruit of your *loom*," Robbie. Elizabeth said, "Blessed is the fruit of your *womb*"!

Robbie: (pause) That's not the same thing, is it?

Name: No, Robbie, I'm afraid it's not.

Robbie: I'm *so* embarrassed.

Name: Robbie, you don't have to be embarrassed. We have these talks together so that we can learn from one another. I don't always understand the readings either.

Robbie: GET OUT! *Really?* But you're so smart and you can read and everything…

Name: That doesn't mean I always understand; I'm still learning just like you. You know, Robbie, we all put on our underwear one leg at a time.

Robbie: Uh…(Name). I don't wear clothes.

Name: Well…(pause), I think we've all learned something new today. So… where were we?

Robbie: The gospel lesson?

Name: Right. Well, it's no wonder we got a little off track this morning. I think we're all pretty excited that this is the last Sunday before…

Robbie: Christmas!

Name: Maybe the excitement we feel today is how Mary and Elizabeth were feeling like in the gospel reading this morning.

Robbie: They were both excited because they were going to have babies!

Name: Elizabeth's baby, John the Baptist, *new life!*

Robbie: And Mary's baby, Jesus, our Christ!

Name: A present for the world!

Robbie: A gift for all ages!

Name: It's hard not to get excited with such *Good News!*

Robbie: It sure is. Uh, (Name), can I be excused?

Name: Sure, Robbie, is everything alright?

Robbie: Amazing! It's just that with all the excitement…I've got to change my shorts. Amen.

Name: Amen.

1ˢᵗ Sunday after Christmas

Luke 2:41–52, MSG

Luke 2:41–45 Every year Jesus' parents traveled to Jerusalem for the Feast of Passover. When he was twelve years old, they went up as they always did for the Feast. When it was over and they left for home, the child Jesus stayed behind in Jerusalem, but his parents didn't know it. Thinking he was somewhere in the company of pilgrims, they journeyed for a whole day and then began looking for him among relatives and neighbors. When they didn't find him, they went back to Jerusalem looking for him.

Name: Good morning and Merry Christmas. I hope everyone is still in the Christmas Spirit! Let's see if Robbie's still got some jingle in his belly! 1, 2, 3…*Robbie!*

Robbie: Where'd he go?

Name: Robbie?

Robbie: He was here just a minute ago…

Name: Robbie!

Robbie: Oh sorry, (Name). I'm just a little frantic. I don't know where he's gone?

Name: Who?

Robbie: Jesus, that's who!

Name: Jesus?

Robbie: Yeah you know, little baby, nestled in a manger, no crying he makes. He was here on Christmas Eve, but now he's gone.

Name: Oh, Robbie. You know, your looking for Jesus reminds me of the gospel lesson for this morning.

Robbie: Really? Well let's keep the chat short, because I've got to keep looking for Jesus.

Name: In the gospel lesson this morning, Mary, Joseph, and Jesus go to Jerusalem to celebrate Passover, but when they were going home, Mary and Joseph noticed that Jesus wasn't with them.

Robbie: He's missing again? What's *with* that kid?

Name: Well, Robbie, Jesus' parents went back to Jerusalem to look for him. They looked everywhere; they asked everyone if they'd seen their boy.

Robbie: Did they put up posters that said, "Have you seen our son: 12 years old, 147 cm, 38.5 kg, slight halo"?

Name: No, Robbie, they didn't. When they got to Jerusalem, they saw that a large crowd had gathered at the temple. So they went to see what was happening and, to their surprise and relief, they saw *Jesus!*

Robbie: What was he doing at the temple?

Name: He was sitting with the teachers, listening and asking questions. The teachers were *very* impressed at the young boy's wisdom.

Robbie: I bet his *parents* were impressed!

Name: Uh…I don't think impressed is the right word. They were *ticked!* Jesus was still just a boy and to go wandering off away from his parents… They were worried sick!

Robbie: Just like I am this morning!

Name: Robbie, you don't have to worry about the baby Jesus. The Bible tells us he grew up, and, as he grew up and closer to God, he had to leave his parents so he could teach *us* how to grow closer to God.

Robbie: So I shouldn't worry?

Name: That's right, because whenever we follow God's way of kindness, compassion, healing, and forgiveness, Jesus is with us – in our hearts and minds, and in our spirit.

Robbie: Okay. You know I'm kinda glad Jesus grew up.

Name: Why's that, Robbie?

Robbie: Diapers.

Name: Say no more!

Robbie: Amen.

2nd Sunday after Christmas

John 1:1–18

1:1 In the beginning was the Word, and the Word was with God, and the Word was God.

1:2 He was in the beginning with God.

1:3 All things came into being through him, and without him not one thing came into being. What has come into being

1:4 in him was life, and the life was the light of all people.

1:5 The light shines in the darkness, and the darkness did not overcome it.

Name: Good morning, everyone! I hope everyone has had a wonderful Christmas season! I wonder how Robbie's Christmas was? Let's call him and see if he can help us with today's lesson. 1, 2, 3...*Robbie!*

Name: Good morning, Robbie.

Robbie: 363. (Substitute with the actual number of days before Christmas.)

Name: 363 what?

Robbie: 363 days till Christmas comes again. We're right back at the beginning.

Name: I know how you feel, Robbie. The weeks leading up to Christmas can be so exciting.

Robbie: That's for sure. Singing Christmas carols...

Name: Lighting the Advent wreath every week getting closer to Christmas.

Robbie: Gathering with family and friends, sharing goodness and joy with the world.

Name: And then...

Robbie: Back to the beginning

Name: Back to the start. You know, Robbie, this reminds me of the gospel lesson this morning.

Robbie: Really?

Name: Really, Robbie. In the gospel this morning, John tells us about the beginning of Christmas.

Robbie: But (Name), we already know about the beginning. The angel's announcing Jesus' birth, Mary and Joseph going to Bethlehem, the Magi who came from the East. Blah, blah, blah...

Name: I know. I thought that was the beginning of Christmas *too*, but the gospel of John tells us Christ came into the world long before Jesus' birth.

Robbie: Really, how long before? A week?

Name: Longer.

Robbie: A month?

Name: Longer than that.

Robbie: A year?

Name: Much, much longer.

Robbie: I give up; how long?

Name: Since the beginning of time, since the beginning of all things. The gospel says, "In the beginning was the Word, and the Word was with God, and the Word was God. He was in the beginning with God. All things came into being through him, and without him not one thing came into being. What has come into being in him was life, and the life was the light of all people. The light shines in the darkness, and the darkness did not overcome it."

Robbie: Wow! That's really the beginning of the beginning! But I'm confused? The gospel says the Word was with us? What is the Word?

Name: Well, Robbie, the Word is God.

Robbie: The Word is God?

Name: That's right, Robbie, and on Christmas we celebrate that the Word became flesh in Jesus.

Robbie: Living, breathing, teaching, healing, flesh and blood. You know, (Name), I'm glad I don't have to wait a whole year for Christmas to come again. I can celebrate Christmas every day.

Name: Let heaven and angels sing! Amen.

Robbie: Amen.

Epiphany Sunday

Matthew 2:1–12, MSG

2:11 [The Magi] entered the house and saw the child in the arms of Mary, his mother. Overcome, they kneeled and worshiped him. Then they opened their luggage and presented gifts: gold, frankincense, myrrh.

Name: Good morning, everyone! It is so great to be here at the start of a New Year! Soon we'll be back to school, back to work, back to whatever it is we do after holidays. I wonder how Robbie is feeling about the New Year? Let's call him and find out. 1, 2, 3…*Robbie!*

Robbie: (Robbie appears with a party hat on his head, shouts out) *Ip, pif, fannie, Ip, pif, fannie!*

Name: Robbie, are you speaking dragon this morning?

Robbie: No, I'm celebrating today with my cheer! *Ip pif fannie! Ip pif fannie!*

Name: Celebrating what? Christmas is over, New Year's Eve is over. What's left to celebrate?

Robbie: (Name), didn't you hear the gospel lesson this morning?

Name: Yes, it's the story of the Magi going to visit the baby Jesus.

Robbie: Exactly, and you know what people do when a baby's born?

Name: Uh… Bring gifts to the parents for the baby?

Robbie: Exactly, that's what the Magi did. What *else* to you do when you find out a baby's been born?

Name: Uh… you congratulate the parents and give thanks for the gift of a child.

Robbie: And that's exactly what I was doing this morning. *Ip,pif, fannie! Ip, pif, fannie!* (Repeat until "Name" interrupts.)

Name: Okay, okay, Robbie. I get it. You want to celebrate like the Magi did when they found the baby Jesus. But I still don't understand your cheer. It kind of sounds like "Hip, hip hurray," which is something people shout at a birthday.

Robbie: Well, maybe in my excitement I'm cheering too quickly. Let's say it slowly, repeat after me. *Ip*

Name: *Ip*

Robbie: *Pif*

Name: *Pif*

Robbie: *Fannie*

Name: *Fannie*

Robbie: Okay, now let's say it altogether a little faster.

Name and Robbie: (together they say ippiffannie like you would a choo, choo train; slowly building up steam) *Ippiffanie, ippiffannie, Ippiffannie…*

Name: Oh, I get it, Robbie. You're cheering Epiphany!

Robbie: You got it! I'm cheering *Ip pif fannie* (Epiphany) because today is Epiphany. Today we celebrate that light has come into the World! The light is Jesus.

Name: The light came into world to show us the way.

Robbie: The way of reaching out to others with kindness, compassion, joy…

Name: Justice, peace, and love.

Robbie: I think it would be great if we all cheered together.

Name: Let's give it a try. Okay, everyone, are you ready? Let's start slow and get faster!

Ip pif fannie, ip pif fannie, ip pif fannie, Epiphany!

Robbie: Amen.

Baptism of Jesus

Luke 3:15–17

3:15 As the people were filled with expectation, and all were questioning in their hearts concerning John, whether he might be the Messiah,

3:16 John answered all of them by saying, "I baptize you with water; but one who is more powerful than I is coming; I am not worthy to untie the thong of his sandals. He will baptize you with the Holy Spirit and fire.

3:17 His winnowing fork is in his hand, to clear his threshing floor and to gather the wheat into his granary; but the chaff he will burn with unquenchable fire."

Name: Good morning, everyone. It's great to be together this morning. Robbie's been acting kind of strange this week. I wonder what's up? Let's call him. 1,2,3…*Robbie!*

Name: Good morning, Robbie.

Robbie: (Name), can you tell me what temperature water freezes at?

Name: Ah… I think it's 0 degrees Celsius.

Robbie: That's what I thought. And what's the temperature outside today?

Name: I don't know, Robbie, maybe around (say the temperature).

Robbie: That settles it. I'm not going in.

Name: "Going in" where?

Robbie: Didn't you listen to the gospel reading this morning?

Name: I sure did. Today we heard about Jesus' baptism. The passage said people were filled with expectation, that John might be the Messiah. John was baptizing people in the river as a symbol of washing out the old and bringing in the new.

Robbie: Brrr. Too cold, and besides, that the river is frozen over. We'd have to drill a hole in the ice! If you haven't noticed (Name), I'm *not* a polar bear.

Name: Oh, Robbie, you don't have to get wet this morning.

Robbie: Really?

Name: Really. Today we tell the story of Jesus' baptism because it marks the beginning of his ministry.

Robbie: The beginning of Jesus' ministry?

Name: That's right. The people in Jesus' day were hoping that God would send someone to show them how to be God's people.

Robbie: And some people thought it was Jesus' cousin, John the Baptist.

Name: That's right. But John said, "Wait, someone is coming who is even *more* filled with the spirit of God than I am."

Robbie: And that someone was Jesus.

Name: That's right, Robbie. Today we remember when Jesus was baptized, and that he was recognized as the "someone" who would show us God's way.

Robbie: So I don't have to get wet this morning.

Name: No.

Robbie: I don't have to worry about catching a cold from being in cold water.

Name: No, Robbie. All you're asked to remember is that when Jesus was baptized he chose to be one of us, and to share the Good News of God's love, God's justice, and God's compassion with the whole world.

Robbie: Okay, well I better get going.

Name: Going where?

Robbie: Well, since I already drilled a hole in the ice I better get fishing.

Name: Oh, Robbie, that's a lesson for another day. Amen.

Robbie: Amen.

2nd Sunday after the Epiphany

John 2:1–11, MSG

2:1–3 Three days later there was a wedding in the village of Cana in Galilee. Jesus' mother was there. Jesus and his disciples were guests also. When they started running low on wine at the wedding banquet, Jesus' mother told him, "They're just about out of wine."

Name: Good morning, everyone. Well I am certainly interested in what Robbie has to say about this week's gospel lesson. Let's see if he's home. 1, 2, 3…*Robbie!*

Name: Good morning, Robbie!

Robbie: Good morning, (Name)!

Name: Well, you're certainly perky this morning, Rob!

Robbie: Well, who *wouldn't* be after hearing this morning's lesson!

Name: You mean the lesson about Jesus going to the wedding.

Robbie: Exactly, (Name)! Because you know what a wedding is?

Name: Well, yes, a wedding is where two people come and share the love they have for one another with all their friends and relatives: young people, old people, aunties, uncles, grandparents, parents, and God are part of it all.

Robbie: Yeah, yeah, I really like those things, but it's what happens after that that I like.

Name: What's that, Robbie?

Robbie: Party! Lots of good things to eat and drink, and then what I love to do the most.

Name: What's that?

Robbie: Dance!

Name: Well, I don't know about the dancing, but a wedding is certainly a celebration. And the gospel lesson this morning reminds us that Jesus…

Robbie: Liked to party!

Name: Robbie, tone it down a bit; we're in church after all.

Robbie: Sorry, (Name). Would it be better if I said Jesus liked to "celebrate"?

Name: Much more dignified, Robbie. Jesus *did* like to celebrate. In fact, I think Jesus' whole life was a celebration of the life God gave us.

Robbie: Really?

Name: Sure, Robbie. When Jesus taught about God's love for all God's people, he was teaching us to share and spread that love to everyone.

Robbie: Jesus was asking everybody to join the party! I mean celebration.

Name: That's right, Robbie. You see, the Kindom of God Jesus talked about was like a wedding celebration with an invitation for everyone.

Robbie: Young people, old people, all languages, all colours, people dressed up and people dressed down: everyone is invited to share God's love with one another.

Name: So when the wine began to run out, it was symbolic of the people's spirit running out.

Robbie: They were forgetting how to celebrate.

Name: That's right! So Jesus' mom gave him a little push and said, "Jesus, this party is dying; get out there and see what you can do!"

Robbie: And boy did he ever get the party started!

Name: He sure did, Robbie, and the great news is that we're all invited to join the celebration today.

Robbie: PAAARTY! Ooops, sorry.

Name: Amen.

Robbie: Amen.

3rd Sunday after the Epiphany

Luke 4:14–21

4:17 and the scroll of the prophet Isaiah was given to him. He unrolled the scroll and found the place where it was written:

4:18 "The Spirit of the Lord is upon me, because he has anointed me to bring good news to the poor. He has sent me to proclaim release to the captives and recovery of sight to the blind, to let the oppressed go free…"

Name: Well, it is so good to see everyone here today! It was soooooo cold this week. I've been *really* worried about Robbie! Should we see if he's home this morning? 1, 2, 3… *Robbie!*

Robbie: (comes out all wrapped up in hat and scarf)

Name: Good morning, Robbie!

Robbie: (mumbles through his scarf covering his mouth)

Name: Oh, Robbie, you're so bundled up I can't understand a word you're saying! Let me help you. There, how's that?

Robbie: Oh thanks so much! I could hardly breathe. Wearing all these winter clothes is such a burden: long underwear, snow pants, extra socks, snow boots, mittens, toques, scarves. I'm so exhausted by the time I'm dressed that I'm too tired to even go out and play!

Name: Well, Robbie, that reminds me of the gospel lesson this morning.

Robbie: You've got to be *joking!* How does getting all dressed up in long underwear, snow pants, extra socks, snow boots, mittens, toques, and scarves have anything to do with the gospel lesson? Did Jesus wear a snowsuit?

Name: No, Robbie, Jesus didn't wear a snow suit!

Robbie: Winter boots?

Name: No.

Robbie: Scarves?

Name: No.

Robbie: Mittens?

Name: No.

Robbie: Long underwear?

Name: Probably not!

Robbie: Well then, what does having to get all dressed up in winter clothes have to do with the gospel lesson?

Name: Well, you know when you said what a burden it was to put all that stuff on?

Robbie: Yes.

Name: Well, the people that Jesus talked to were feeling burdened, too. Their clothes weren't a burden, but their lives were very difficult.

Robbie: Like when I get three pages of math homework that's due the next day!

Name: It can feel like a burden.

Robbie: Or you're sick and you've got no one to help you get better?

Name: It can feel very heavy.

Robbie: Or when you're hungry and there is no one to help you prepare a meal.

Name: It can be very hard.

Robbie: When there are so many rules that you feel you can't breathe!

Name: That's it, Robbie. When Jesus came to the synagogue, which was kind of like our church, he was handed a scroll from the Hebrew Bible, what we call the Old Testament, so he could read from the book of Isaiah, which began…

Robbie: "God's Spirit is on me; he's chosen me to preach the Message of good news to the poor, Sent me to announce pardon to prisoners and recovery of sight to the blind, To set the burdened and battered free, to announce, 'This is God's year to act!'"

Name: Then he rolled up the scroll, handed it back to the assistant, and sat down. Everybody in the church looked at him! And he said, "You've just heard Scripture make history. It came true just now in this place."

Robbie: So Jesus was the one who tried to set people free from their burdens.

Name: That's right, Robbie. Jesus was saying now is the time to help each other with our burdens.

Robbie: Care for one another!

Name: Love one another.

Robbie: Forgive one another.

Name: That's it, Robbie!

Robbie: Well, maybe you can help me!

Name: How can I do that?

Robbie: Could you bundle me up in my scarf again? It's cold in the castle.

Name: Happy to help, Robbie. Amen.

Robbie: (scarf on) hmphm, hmph!

4ᵗʰ Sunday after the Epiphany

Jeremiah 1:4–10, NRSV

11:8 "Do not be afraid of them, for I am with you to deliver you, says the LORD."

11:9 Then the LORD put out his hand and touched my mouth; and the LORD said to me, "Now I have put my words in your mouth."

Name: Good morning, everyone! I'm sure everyone is waiting to hear what Robbie has to say about today's lesson. Let's call him out. 1, 2, 3… *Robbie!*

Name: Good morning, Robbie.

Robbie: Good morning.

Name: What do you have to say for yourself?

Robbie: I'm sort of afraid to say anything, (Name).

Name: Really, Robbie? That's not like you.

Robbie: I know. Usually I've got no problem talking. Just wind me up and I'm quite the chatterbox.

Name: So what's happened?

Robbie: Well, I just realized something.

Name: What's that?

Robbie: People might actually listen to what I say.

Name: And?

Robbie: And it's frightening. I mean, who am I? I'm just a lowly dragon talking about God. I mean who am I to talk about God?

Name: You know, Robbie, you remind me of Jeremiah.

Robbie: Jemimah? Do you want some *pancakes*?

Name: No, Robbie, the *prophet* Jeremiah, not the *pancake* Jemimah. In the lesson today, God asks *Jeremiah* to speak about God's hope for God's people.

Robbie: Oh my, I think it might have been easier if God had asked Jeremiah to make pancakes.

Name: Maybe, Robbie, but God wanted Jeremiah to speak to the people about God's vision for the people of Israel.

Robbie: That's frightening, speaking for God.

Name: Well, that's how Jeremiah felt. Jeremiah didn't think he could speak for God. After all, he was just a kid.

Robbie: That's what I'm saying, (Name). I'm big for my age, but I'm just a baby dragon. How can I speak about God?

Name: But God said to Jeremiah, "Don't say, 'I'm only a boy.' I'll tell you where to go and you'll go there. I'll tell you what to say and you'll say it. Don't be afraid of a soul. I'll be right there, looking after you."

Robbie: And Jeremiah spoke to the people about God?

Name: He did, and the people listened. I know it can be frightening speaking out. We might be afraid people won't listen to us when we speak out about injustice.

Robbie: Like the time I told my friends to stop picking on the smallest person in my class.

Name: You did that, Robbie?

Robbie: I sure did.

Name: Where did you get the courage?

Robbie: I guess I got it from God. Every Sunday when we talk, I know more and more about God, and about who and how God wants us to be. It's like God put the words in my mouth and in my heart and I wasn't afraid.

Name: I think that's it, Robbie. Every week we remind each other how God wants us to live with one another. So when we see things that are not loving, or caring, we can speak out.

Robbie: You know, (Name), there's something else that helps.

Name: What's that?

Robbie: It helps to have a script.

Name: Amen.

Robbie: Amen.

5ᵗʰ Sunday after the Epiphany

Luke 5:1–11, NRSV

5:4 When he had finished speaking, he said to Simon, "Put out into the deep water and let down your nets for a catch."

Name: Good morning, everyone. I'm sure glad to be here this morning and I'm really looking forward to a visit from Robbie. Let's call him shall we? 1, 2, 3... *Robbie!*

Name: Good morning, Robbie!

Robbie: Arye! (like a pirate with an eye patch) Are ye ready, Matey?

Name: Are we ready for what?

Robbie: Are ye ready to get in the boat?

Name: What boat?

Robbie: Hoist the main sail, trim the jib, swab the poop deck... You know, (Name), I'm afraid to ask why we need to mop up the poop deck? Anyway, anchors away!

Name: Robbie, I'm afraid to tell you this, but we're not on a boat.

Robbie: We're not?

Name: No, we're not.

Robbie: Are we going to get in a boat?

Name: Not this morning.

Robbie: Well then, I guess the gospel reading for this today is totally useless. And here I spent a dollar fifty on this cool eye patch!

Name: Well, Robbie, you can keep the eye patch and you can keep the lesson for this morning.

Robbie: Really?

Name: Of course! Do you know why Jesus went out into the boat?

Robbie: The buses were full?

Name: No, Robbie, he got in a boat because the people were crowded by the shore of the lake. It was so crowded that people couldn't see or hear what Jesus was teaching.

Robbie: So Jesus wanted to get in the boat, go out on the lake so everyone could see and hear him.

Name: That's right. He asked Simon, who later was known as Peter, if he could take him just offshore so he could speak to all the people.

Robbie: And Peter did? Even after he fished all night and was tired and probably wanted to go home and sleep.

Name: Even after being up all night, Peter was excited to hear what Jesus had to say.

Robbie: What did he say?

Name: Well, the lesson this morning doesn't tell us exactly what Jesus said, but I imagine he said the same things we hear in other lessons.

Robbie: Like, teaching lessons of God's love for everyone?

Name: I think so.

Robbie: Teaching that God wants us to take care of the sick, the lonely, and the poor?

Name: Good lessons to teach.

Robbie: Teaching us that God forgives us when we make mistakes.

Name: Sounds good.

Robbie: Teaching us that by loving our neighbours we're showing love to God.

Name: And…?

Robbie: And what?

Name: Teaching us one other very important lesson.

Robbie: Which is…

Name: How to fish.

Robbie: I knew it! We *do* need a boat, or at least a lake, or a river, even a mud puddle.

Name: Not how to fish for fish, but how to fish for people.

Robbie: Fish for people? Don't I need a special licence for that?

Name: You've already got one, Robbie.

Robbie: Don't I need some kind of fancy bait?

Name: You've got all the bait you need.

Robbie: Don't I need a big net?

Name: God has given you the biggest net you need. If you want to fish like Jesus, all you need to do is cast your net of love out into the world.

Robbie: If I want to fish like Jesus, I need to lure people towards loving one another.

Name: When you were born, God gave you a licence to be a fisher of goodness, and of kindness.

Robbie: A fisher of justice and peace.

Name: Amen.

Robbie: (Name), one more thing: Anchors away! Let's get fishing. Amen.

6ᵗʰ Sunday after the Epiphany

Luke 6:17–26, NRSV

6:18 They had come to hear him and to be healed of their diseases; and those who were troubled with unclean spirits were cured.

6:19 And all in the crowd were trying to touch him, for power came out from him and healed all of them.

6:20 Then he looked up at his disciples and said: "Blessed are you who are poor, for yours is the kingdom of God."

Name: Good morning, everyone. I'm sure glad to be here this morning and I'm really looking forward to a visit from Robbie. Let's call him shall we? 1, 2, 3… *Robbie!*

Name: Good morning, Robbie.

Robbie: No pain, no gain!

Name: What's that, Robbie?

Robbie: No pain, no gain!

Name: Oh. You know who said that don't you?

Robbie: I sure do.

Name: It was…

Robbie: Jesus!

Name: Jesus?

Robbie: Sure!

Name: Robbie, Arnold Schwarzenegger said that.

Robbie: Arnold Schwarzenegger, a.k.a. the Terminator/turned Governor?

Name: Well, he said it while he was a body builder…but, yes… *that* Arnold… He was talking about building up your body. It's hard work, but it's worth it: "No pain, no gain."

Robbie: Funny, it sounds kinda messed up.

Name: How so, Robbie?

Robbie: Like two opposites. Pain is a bad thing. Gain is a good thing. They don't go together. They're topsy-turvy.

Name: I see.

Robbie: Like what Jesus said in today's gospel reading.

Name: Oh, that's why you thought Jesus said "No pain, no gain."

Robbie: Sure… I mean, it sounds like something he might say.

Name: Like "Happy are the poor."

Robbie: Right! What's so happy about being poor?

Name: And "Happy are those who mourn."

Robbie: Those really sound opposite! Mourning and happiness don't go together.

Name: Or "Blessed are you when you are persecuted."

Robbie: That doesn't sound like a blessing. I wouldn't feel very blessed if someone beat me up, or made fun of me, or killed me.

Name: I think Jesus was looking at things in a different way, Robbie.

Robbie: Really?

Name: Jesus was talking about God's children…

Robbie: Like you and me?

Name: And all the people here. Yes.

Robbie: Are *we* going to be poor? Is there a cut in the puppet budget, (Name)?

Name: Not that I know of.

Robbie: Are we going to mourn, are we going to persecuted, or made fun of?

Name: Well maybe, Robbie; I hope not, but maybe so.

Robbie: That's awful!

Name: But it's not, Robbie. That's what Jesus was talking about.

Robbie: Huh?

Name: God's children are *always* blessed… are *always* fortunate.

Robbie: Why?

Name: Because we are God's children!

Robbie: *Oh!*

Name: And being God's children – being blessed and loved by God – helps us get through all the other stuff, even when it's bad stuff.

Robbie: So they aren't opposites – being happy and being poor, being happy and mourning, being persecuted and…

Name: God's children are *always* blessed. In all things, God is with us in the good, the bad, and…..

Robbie: Don't' tell me… *Clint Eastwood!*

Name: Say goodbye, Robbie.

Robbie: *Hasta la vista*, Baby.

7ᵗʰ Sunday after the Epiphany

Luke 6:27–38

6:27 "But I say to you that listen, Love your enemies, do good to those who hate you,

6:28 bless those who curse you, pray for those who abuse you.

6:29 If anyone strikes you on the cheek, offer the other also; and from anyone who takes away your coat do not withhold even your shirt.

6:30 Give to everyone who begs from you; and if anyone takes away your goods, do not ask for them again.

6:31 Do to others as you would have them do to you."

Name: Good morning, everyone. I'm really glad to be here this morning and I am really looking forward to chatting with Robbie about today's lesson. Let's call him. 1, 2, 3... *Robbie!*

Name: Good morning, Robbie.

Robbie: Hit me!

Name: Excuse me?

Robbie: Call me a dumb dragon.

Name: *What?*

Robbie: Take my coat.

Name: Robbie, you're not wearing a coat.

Robbie: How about my castle. Maybe you'd like to move in?

Name: Robbie, what's got into you this morning?

Robbie: The gospel lesson.

Name: The gospel lesson?

Robbie: Yes. Jesus said that if you want to follow him you've got to be a punching bag.

Name: I don't think that's exactly what Jesus was saying.

Robbie: Jesus said, if you want to follow me, you've got let people curse you.

Name: Robbie, that's *not* what Jesus is saying.

Robbie: If you want to be my disciple, you've got to let someone steal your coat!

Name: Robbie, I don't think that's what Jesus meant.

Robbie: Well, that's a relief; I don't much like the thought of people picking on me.

Name: You know, Robbie, I think what Jesus was trying to say is that if someone is mean to you, don't turn around and be mean to that person.

Robbie: That sounds like Jesus. Jesus always wanted people to try to be loving, even when we didn't *feel* like being loving.

Name: Jesus was telling his friends, if someone calls you names, don't turn around and call *them* names.

Robbie: That sounds like Jesus – calling someone names doesn't make anyone feel better.

Name: You know, Robbie, I don't know anyone who hasn't been hurt by someone else, either by being picked on or bullied. Sometimes we feel so bad we want to hurt them in return. But Jesus said that the way to feel better is not to hurt someone else, but to love them.

Robbie: Love them?

Name: That's right. Treat others the way you would like to be treated.

Robbie: I like to be treated with kindness.

Name: So we treat others with kindness.

Robbie: I like people to speak nicely to me.

Name: So we speak nicely to others.

Robbie: I don't like to be hit.

Name: So we don't hit others.

Robbie: Hug me!

Name: That's something I can do.

Robbie: Amen.

8ᵗʰ Sunday after the Epiphany

Luke 6:39–49

6:41 "Why do you see the speck in your neighbor's eye, but do not notice the log in your own eye?

6:42 Or how can you say to your neighbor, 'Friend, let me take out the speck in your eye,' when you yourself do not see the log in your own eye? You hypocrite, first take the log out of your own eye, and then you will see clearly to take the speck out of your neighbor's eye."

Name: Good morning, everyone! It's great to be here this morning. I wonder what Robbie has to say about the lesson this morning. Let's call him. 1, 2, 3… *Robbie!*

Name: Good morning, Robbie!

Robbie: Good morning. Can you stand a little closer, (Name)? I can't see you very well.

Name: Sure, Robbie, how's this?

Robbie: A little better, but you're still kind of blurry.

Name: Wow, Robbie. Do you think you should get your eyes checked?

Robbie: I did. That's what got me in trouble.

Name: How did getting your eyes checked get you in trouble? Who's your eye doctor?

Robbie: Jesus.

Name: Jesus?

Robbie: Didn't you hear the gospel lesson for this morning?

Name: I *thought* I did.

Robbie: Well, (Name), this morning Jesus is teaching people all about eye surgery.

Name: Uh, Robbie, I don't think…

Robbie: When you notice your friend has something in their eye…

Name: Robbie?

Robbie: Don't just grab a pair of tweezers and start fishing around…

Name: Robbie?

Robbie: Because you've probably got a big stick in your own eye…

Name: Robbie, stop! Not only are you not seeing well this morning, I think something is wrong with your hearing.

Robbie: What?

Name: Exactly. When Jesus was telling people to make sure they see clearly before they start telling *other* people how to see, Jesus was telling people *not* to tell others how to live before they think about how *they* are living.

Robbie: Oh, I see.

Name: Really?

Robbie: No, you've lost me completely!

Name: Okay, here's an example. Let's say you're in the playground.

Robbie: Are there any logs in the playground?

Name: No, Robbie, there are no logs.

Robbie: Any sticks or specks?

Name: Robbie!

Robbie: Sorry, please continue.

Name: Okay, you're in the playground and you're telling someone else to share the ball because they are not sharing; they're just keeping it to themselves.

Robbie: Not Fair!

Name: Exactly. But then the person with the ball says to you, "Well, last recess you kept the ball the whole time and you didn't share at all!"

Robbie: Ouch.

Name: You see, you didn't notice that you were being unkind when you didn't share, but you sure noticed it when someone *else* wasn't sharing.

Robbie: So Jesus was telling people they have to notice how they are acting before they criticize others.

Name: That's right. Jesus was talking about the leaders who were criticizing people for not following God's way.

Robbie: To be just, to be kind, to be caring, to be compassionate and forgiving.

Name: Jesus told the leaders that they had to think about whether or not *they* were following God's way *themselves*!

Robbie: Get the logs out of their own eyes!

Name: That's it, Robbie.

Robbie: Thanks for clearing things up about today's lesson. I've got to run.

Name: Run? Where you going?

Robbie: I'm booked for heart surgery.

Name: Oh, Robbie. Amen.

9th Sunday after the Epiphany

Luke 7:1–10

7:6 And Jesus went with them, but when he was not far from the house, the centurion sent friends to say to him, "Lord, do not trouble yourself, for I am not worthy to have you come under my roof";

Name: Good morning, everyone. Well, this is the last Sunday of Epiphany! I sure hope Robbie has some Good News to share with us. Let's call him. 1, 2, 3… *Robbie!*

Name: Good morning, Robbie.

Robbie: Who turned off the lights?

Name: What are you talking about, Robbie; there's plenty of light here this morning.

Robbie: No, I mean, who turned off the lights?

Name: What light are you talking about?

Robbie: You said this is the last Sunday of Epiphany. Epiphany is the season of light. Are you telling me that after this Sunday the Light of the world is turned off?

Name: Oh, I see what you mean, Robbie. You're afraid that when the season of Epiphany is over, Jesus – the light of the world – will be gone too?

Robbie: Who pulled the plug?

Name: Robbie, no one's pulling the plug. Epiphany is the season when we celebrate and remember Jesus, the light of the world, coming to us. But even though the season ends, the light is still with us.

Robbie: That's a relief. For a minute I thought maybe someone forgot to pay the electric bill and we weren't worthy of the light anymore.

Name: You know, Robbie, this conversation reminds me of the gospel lesson this morning.

Robbie: Keep it light.

Name: I'll try. This morning we heard about Jesus arriving into a town called Capernaum. No sooner had he arrived and he gets a message.

Robbie: Oh boy, I could really do with a massage.

Name: Not a *massage,* Robbie, a *message.* The message was from a soldier who was concerned about one of his servants who was sick. The soldier had heard about how Jesus was a great healer and he hoped Jesus would come and make his servant better.

Robbie: Visiting the sick, that sounds like something Jesus would do.

Name: It sure does and Jesus was on his way to visit the sick person when he got another message.

Robbie: Another message?

Name: Friends of the soldier met Jesus when he was close to the soldier's house and they told Jesus that the soldier didn't think he was *good* enough for Jesus to come to his house.

Robbie: How come he didn't think he was good enough?

Name: Maybe it was because he was a Roman soldier and he didn't think Jesus would bother with someone who wasn't Jewish like Jesus was.

Robbie: *That* doesn't sound like Jesus. Jesus taught that we are *all* God's people and God cares for us no matter *who* we are.

Name: You're right, Robbie.

Robbie: Did you say I'm light?

Name: Well, I *kind* of did. You see, Jesus was light to the world. Jesus showed up in dark places where people were sick, or lonely, or sad.

Robbie: Jesus showed up to lighten people's lives by letting them know that God loves them and that *he* loved them.

Name: You know, Robbie, we carry that *same* light with us into the world. Just because Epiphany is over doesn't mean lights out, because *nothing* can put out the light of God's love for the whole world and for us.

Robbie: That's Good News.

Name: It sure is. Amen.

Last Sunday after the Epiphany

Transfiguration Sunday

Luke 9:28–36

9:28–31 About eight days after saying this, he climbed the mountain to pray, taking Peter, John, and James along. While he was in prayer, the appearance of his face changed and his clothes became blinding white. At once two men were there talking with him. They turned out to be Moses and Elijah – and what a glorious appearance they made! They talked over his exodus, the one Jesus was about to complete in Jerusalem.

Two scripts have been provided for this week. Use the first script if Transfiguration Sunday falls on or near February 14 and you would like to make explicit reference to Valentine's Day.

Script 1 (Valentine's Day)

Name: Good morning, everyone. It's great to be here with you this morning. You know, I feel awful because I forgot to send Robbie a Valentine's Day card. But I've got these hearts and I was hoping you'd help me put them on Robbie's castle as a Valentine. Will you help me? 1, 2, 3… *Robbie!*

Robbie: Good morning, everyone. Good morning, (Name).

Name: Good morning, Robbie.

Robbie: (Name).

Name: Robbie!

Robbie: What?

Name: Don't you have something to say to everyone and to me?

Robbie: Oh yeah right, (Name). Floss: it's very important that you floss. If you notice, *my* teeth…

Name: No, Robbie, look at your castle. Didn't you notice all the hearts on your castle?

Robbie: Oh, (Name), I *didn't* notice all the hearts. They're *beautiful.*

Name: Well, Robbie, it's our way of saying, we love you!

Robbie: Oh, (Name), that's beautiful and you know it works so much better than other special church days.

Name: Like what?

Robbie: Well, for example, it's better than wishing somebody a happy Transfiguration Sunday.

Name: A what?

Robbie: Transfiguration Sunday. You know, (Name). Today is the day we remember the story of Jesus and his friends Peter, James, and John, when they climbed a mountain. They were taking a break from all the work they had been doing.

Name: Oh right, Robbie. They climbed the mountain and when they got to the top they were tired and so some of them fell asleep.

Robbie: But not Jesus.

Name: No, not Jesus. Jesus stayed awake and was praying and then the story says that two other figures appeared on the mountain: Moses and Elijah.

Robbie: Hold the phone, (Name)! Moses and Elijah? Those guys lived long before Jesus did.

Name: That's true, Robbie. But, on the mountain, Jesus and Peter felt very close to their ancestors. It was like talking to long-lost friends. And Moses and Elijah told Jesus that God loved him and he was doing a great job preaching and teaching about the Kindom of God.

Robbie: In fact, they were so happy to see Moses and Elijah and to have their blessing that Peter, James, and John never wanted to leave the mountain. They wanted to pitch their tents and just stay there forever.

Name: That's true, but Jesus knew that they couldn't stay on that mountain forever. Jesus knew that he was called to go back down the mountain and to continue teaching, and healing.

Robbie: What a bummer! It reminds me of what happened on Valentine's Day (or "last Valentine's Day," if Valentine's Day has not arrived yet).

Name: What happened?

Robbie: Nothing! Just the same old thing. No chocolates, no roses, no breakfast in…

Name: Hold on, Robbie. It's true that special days come and go. But let's say you're having a bad day and you think that you don't have anyone who cares about you, or that you don't think you matter. Maybe on those days you can remember the hearts on your castle.

Robbie: My transfiguration/valentine's hearts.

Name: That's right, Robbie. Amen.

Robbie: And my heart will be refilled. Amen.

* * *

Script 2

Name: Good morning, everyone. It's great to be here with you this morning. Do you know what special day it is today? No? Well it's Transfiguration Sunday! I looked all over for a "Happy Transfiguration Sunday" card to send Robbie, but I couldn't find any. I guess the card shop must have been all sold out. Even though I couldn't find a card, I've got these hearts and I was hoping you'd help me put them on Robbie's castle as a surprise. Will you help me? 1, 2, 3… *Robbie!*

Robbie: Good morning everyone. Good morning, (Name).

Name: Good morning, Robbie.

Robbie: (Name).

Name: Robbie!

Robbie: What?

Name: Don't you have something to say to me and to everyone else?

Robbie: Oh yeah, right (Name). Floss: It's very important that you floss. If you notice, *my* teeth…

Name: No, Robbie, look at your castle! Didn't you notice all the hearts on your castle?

Robbie: Oh, (Name), I *didn't* notice all the hearts. They're *beautiful*. But, (Name), why are they there?

Name: They're "Happy Transfiguration Sunday" hearts!

Robbie: Transfiguration Sunday Hearts?

Name: Yeah, Transfiguration Sunday. You know, Robbie. Today is the day we remember the story of Jesus and his friends Peter, James, and John, when they climbed a mountain. They were taking a break from all the work they had been doing.

Robbie: Oh right. They climbed the mountain and when they got to the top they were tired and so some of them fell asleep.

Name: But not Jesus. Jesus stayed awake and was praying and then the story says that two other figures appeared on the mountain: Moses and Elijah.

Robbie: Hold the phone, (Name)! Moses and Elijah? Those guys lived way before Jesus did.

Name: That's true, Robbie. But on the mountain Jesus and Peter felt very close to their ancestors. It was like talking to a long-lost friend. And their friends Moses and Elijah told Jesus that God loved him and he was doing a great job preaching and teaching about the Kindom of God.

Robbie: In fact, they were *so* happy to see Moses and Elijah and to have their blessing that Peter, James, and John never wanted to leave the mountain. They wanted to pitch their tents and just stay there forever.

Name: That's true. Jesus knew that they couldn't stay on that mountain forever. Jesus knew that he was called to go back down the mountain to continue teaching and healing, helping to transform the world into God's wonderful Kindom.

Robbie: You know, Name, I think I understand how Jesus' friends felt. Sometimes if I'm having a really special day, I never want it to end. I want it to go on forever!

Name: Sometimes I feel the same way. That's why it's so important to remember special days when your heart was full and you felt the love of God. It's especially important when you're having a bad day and think that you don't have anyone who cares about you, or when you don't think you matter. Maybe on those days you can remember the hearts on your castle and how you are so loved.

Robbie: Remember my transfiguration hearts.

Name: That's right, Robbie. Amen.

Robbie: And my heart will be refilled! Amen.

Lent 1

Luke 4:1–13

4:1 Jesus, full of the Holy Spirit, returned from the Jordan and was led by the Spirit in the wilderness…

Name: Good morning, everyone! Well, it is great to be here this morning. Today we move into a whole new season of the church year. I wonder if Robbie knows what it is? Let's ask him. 1, 2, 3…*Robbie!*

Name: Good morning, Robbie. Today is the beginning of a new church season; do you know what it is?

Robbie: Ah? Pancake season.

Name: No, Robbie. Pancakes are what we sometimes eat before the season starts.

Robbie: Sausage season?

Name: No, Robbie this season has nothing to do with food.

Robbie: Then I guess it's not maple syrup season.

Name: No, Robbie, it's Lent.

Robbie: Oh, I'm afraid I'm not going to like this season.

Name: Why not?

Robbie: Well, remember last year I had a lot of leaves to rake up and I didn't have a rake?

Name: I remember, Robbie. Last year I lent you my rake.

Robbie: And remember last winter when a tree fell down on my castle and you lent me your chainsaw?

Name: I remember going to the hospital with you!

Robbie: Well, I'm afraid I'm not very good at lent because I forgot to return your rake and your saw.

Name: Well, Robbie, it would be great if you returned my rake and my saw, but that's not what the season of Lent is about.

Robbie: It's not?

Name: The season of Lent is the six weeks or 40 days where we remember Jesus being led by the Spirit into the wilderness.

Robbie: Why would the Spirit lead Jesus into the wilderness?

Name: Well, Robbie, sometimes we need to get away from the hustle and bustle of everyday life.

Robbie: Like a vacation?

Name: Kind of, but a very *special* type of vacation. A vacation where we have time to think about our lives, about our relationships with one another, and about who God is calling us to be.

Robbie: And that's what Jesus did?

Name: It sure was. Jesus was led by the Spirit out into the wilderness, and in the wilderness Jesus had time to grow closer to God. His Spirit was refreshed so that he could come back to the world to preach and teach the Good News of God's love.

Robbie: Wow, that sounds great! But my mom won't let me go into the wilderness on my own.

Name: Well, Robbie, maybe we can create our *own* wilderness. We can spend time each day quietly thinking about who God is calling us to be.

Robbie: Can I make a tent in my room?

Name: Uh, sure, Robbie. And maybe in that tent you could invite God to be with you.

Robbie: Can I take some crayons in the tent?

Name: Sure, and maybe you could draw or write some of ways God is in your life.

Robbie: You know, (Name), Lent doesn't sound too bad; it actually sounds like a special time to be with God. But I have a favour to ask.

Name: What's that, Robbie?

Robbie: Can you lend me a red crayon? I can't find mine.

Name: Sure thing, Robbie; it's a lot less dangerous than a chainsaw!

Robbie: Amen.

Lent 2

Luke 13:31–35

13:34 Jerusalem, Jerusalem, the city that kills the prophets and stones those who are sent to it! How often have I desired to gather your children together as a hen gathers her brood under her wings, and you were not willing!

Name: Good morning, everyone. Welcome to the second Sunday of Lent. I hope Robbie has figured out what Lent is all about. Let's call him okay? 1, 2, 3... *Robbie!*

Robbie: (makes chicken sounds)

Name: Ah, Robbie, are you there?

Robbie: Nope, it's just us chickens.

Name: You know, you chickens sound a lot like Robbie.

Robbie: Really! Oh there's no fooling you, (Name). (Robbie comes out)

Name: That's better; you had me worried for a minute. Robbie, why were you pretending to be a chicken this morning?

Robbie: I was pretending to be a chicken because of the gospel lesson.

Name: The gospel lesson?

Robbie: In the gospel lesson, the friends of Jesus are all afraid of King Herod. They're afraid that King Herod's going to chop off their heads just like chickens.

Name: Oh my, that does sound scary. What did Jesus do?

Robbie: Well you know Jesus; he's no chicken!

Name: Well, Robbie, according to the gospel lesson this morning Jesus *is* a chicken.

Robbie: (chicken sound with a question mark) *Bawk?*

Name: Well, at least he's *like* a chicken. In the lesson today, Jesus says he's like a mother hen. A hen is a mama chicken. And mother chickens take care of their baby chicks by spreading their wings and, when they are afraid, all the little chicks can take shelter under her wings.

Robbie: That sounds cozy.

Name: It sure does, but sometimes we're like little chicks that don't listen to our mother, or we don't pay attention. We run around and sometimes we get in trouble.

Robbie: Like the people in Jerusalem we heard about this morning?

Name: That's right. Jesus loved the people so much that he tried to teach them about God's way. He tried to teach them about God's kindom ways of forgiveness, justice, compassion, and peace, but...

Robbie: But the chicks, I mean the people, wouldn't listen.

Name: And that made Jesus sad, because he wanted *everyone* to know about the love of God for all people. He was sad when people would hurt one another.

Robbie: So what about us chickens, I mean people?

Name: Well, Robbie, Jesus still wants to teach us how to be God's children. Jesus wants us to gather around and learn about loving our neighbours as ourselves.

Robbie: Loving God by caring for all God's creatures.

Name: Amen.

Robbie: Cock-a-doodle do unto others as you would have them do unto you!

Lent 3

Luke 13:1–9

13:7 "So he said to the gardener, 'See here! For three years I have come looking for fruit on this fig tree, and still I find none. Cut it down! Why should it be wasting the soil?'

13:8 He replied, 'Sir, let it alone for one more year, until I dig around it and put manure on it.

13:9 If it bears fruit next year, well and good; but if not, you can cut it down.'"

Name: Good morning, everyone. It's great to see everyone here this morning. I wonder how Robbie has been this week. Let's call and see if he's home. 1, 2, 3…*Robbie!*

Name: Oh, Robbie! (Holds nose) What's that smell?

Robbie: Do you like it? It's my new cologne: "o de" gospel.

Name: Your "o de" gospel? It smells like you should "o de" shower!

Robbie: But (Name), I was just doing what Jesus said to do in the gospel lesson for this morning.

Name: This morning's gospel was about a fig tree.

Robbie: But not just *any* old fig tree. A fig tree that didn't grow figs!

Name: So the man who planted the fig tree went to the gardener to ask if he had any tips on how to get that fig tree to grow figs?

Robbie: And the gardener said, "Leave it alone for one more year and I'll dig around it and put…"

Name: "Manure on it!" Oh, Robbie, you *didn't*?

Robbie: I sure did! Last week I got a whole lot of manure for the church. The minister is always going on about growing in our faith but (he/she) forgot to tell us about using fertilizer! You know, (Name), I think I've got just the thing to help you grow. If you just come over here, I can rub some manure on you.

Name: *No thanks!* You know, Robbie, I don't think Jesus meant we were to put manure on us. But Jesus told us what we need to feed our faith.

Robbie: But I thought manure was a good thing?

Name: It's a good food for *plants!* Not such a good thing for people. The kind of fertilizers we need to grow as disciples are usually odourless.

Robbie: Odourless?

Name: Reading the stories in the Bible.

Robbie: That's food for thought.

Name: Caring for others.

Robbie: That's soul food.

Name: Coming together to worship, to pray...

Robbie: And sing.

Name: These things all feed our spirit.

Robbie: So hearing the stories of our faith, worshipping together, sharing with others, caring for others, these are the spiritual fertilizers that help us grow as followers of Jesus.

Name: That's right, and you know what, Robbie?

Robbie: What?

Name: Sometimes you're just full of it!

Robbie: Amen to that.

Lent 4

Luke 15:1–3, 11b–32, MSG

15:1–3 By this time a lot of men and women of doubtful reputation were hanging around Jesus, listening intently. The Pharisees and religion scholars were not pleased, not at all pleased. They growled, "He takes in sinners and eats meals with them, treating them like old friends." Their grumbling triggered this story.

Name: Good morning, everyone! It is great to be there this morning! Let's call out Robbie so he can share this wonderful day with us! 1, 2, 3… *Robbie!*

Name: Good morning, Robbie!

Robbie: Good morning.

Name: Robbie, is that the best you can do? Isn't it great to be here?

Robbie: (sarcastically) Oh yeah, just great.

Name: Robbie, you don't seem very enthusiastic to be here this morning. Is everything all right?

Robbie: Oh yeah, everything's fine.

Name: Robbie?

Robbie: What? (sounding a little angry)

Name: It doesn't sound like everything's all right. What's going on?

Robbie: Well, it's just…it's just, it's…

Name: What?

Robbie: It's just not *fair!*

Name: What's not fair?

Robbie: The gospel reading this morning! It's not fair!

Name: Wow, Robbie, you certainly are upset.

Robbie: Yes I am. Jesus tells the story about two brothers.

Name: A younger brother and an older brother. The younger brother goes to his dad and says…

Robbie: "Dad, I'm outta here. This place is so boring. I want to go out into the world. I don't want to go to bed at 9:30, I'm sick of you telling me to turn off the computer, and I'm sick of having to eat my vegetables. Give me what you'd leave me if you were dead."

Name: Ouch! That must have really made the father sad.

Robbie: It sure did; the father loved his son so much. But the dad said, "Okay, if that's how you feel I'll give you all your inheritance now!"

Name: And then the younger son went with all the money he was given and he spent it on parties and fast camels, fancy clothes, and fancy restaurants. But when the money ran out, so did his friends, and the *fast camels were repossessed*, he found himself with nothing to eat, no place to stay, and…

Robbie: Finally the youngest son realized that he'd made a mess of things; he finally started to understand that the most important things in life are…

Name: The love and care his father offered him…

Robbie: So the youngest son decided to turn his life around, go home, and beg for his father's forgiveness. Just let him sleep in the garage or in the backyard, he would be happy if he just eat whatever was thrown out in the green bin!

Name: But to everyone's surprise (and I do mean you too, Robbie!), the father saw his lost son coming down the road and ran to meet him. Before the son could even beg his father's forgiveness, the father gathered him in a great big bear hug and smothered him with kisses, tears running down his cheeks. He was so happy he yelled for the whole world to hear! "My son was lost and now he is found! *Let's party!*"

Robbie: Now the older brother! The good brother, the dutiful brother, the one who never raised his voice, the one who never forgot to take out the trash, the one who did whatever his father asked him to do. He shouted "It's not fair!" I mean, he did *everything* his dad asked of him. But *he* didn't get a party!

Name: Robbie, is that why you're upset? You don't think it's fair that the father had a big party for the younger son?

Robbie: Bingo!

Name: Not now, Robbie, we're in the middle of a conversation.

Robbie: No, (Name)! Not bingo, the game. I mean that's it exactly! "It's not fair!"

Name: Well, Robbie, here's the thing about God. God's not fair!

Robbie: God's not fair?

Name: Nope. At least, not fair in the way *we* often think is fair. God's love is not fair because God's deepest desire is that we love God and that we learn how to love one another, not counting the cost.

Robbie: So the youngest son lost his way…

Name: And the older son lost his way *too*.

Robbie: But the youngest son found his way back.

Name: And the father's greatest hope was that the older son would find his way back, too.

Robbie: You know what, (Name), I'm *glad* that God's not fair.

Name: Me too. Amen.

Lent 5

John 12:1–8

12:1 Six days before the Passover Jesus came to Bethany, the home of Lazarus, whom he had raised from the dead.

12:2 There they gave a dinner for him. Martha served, and Lazarus was one of those at the table with him.

Name: Good morning, everyone! It is great to be here this morning. And it's so nice that spring is in the air. Let's see if Robbie is home this morning and will come and have a chat with us. 1, 2, 3...*Robbie !*

Robbie: Good morning, (Name)!

Name: Good morning, Robbie, you certainly are chipper this morning Robbie.

Robbie: I sure am, the birds are singing, the snow is melting. I'm putting away my winter boots, my mittens, my snow pants, and my toque!

Name: Well yes, Robbie, spring is sure a welcome sight, it feels like we can relax a bit and let our hair down.

Robbie: Uh, (Name)?

Name: Yes, Robbie?

Robbie: I'm a dragon. We don't have hair.

Name: Oh sorry, Robbie, but letting your hair down is just an expression, it means we can relax and be ourselves without having to worry about what other people think.

Robbie: Oh I see. Well "letting your hair down" does remind me of the gospel lesson this morning.

Name: Really, Robbie, how's that?

Robbie: Well, in the gospel lesson this morning, Jesus gathered with his closest friends...

Name: You mean the apostles: James 1 and James 2, John, Judas, Peter, Andrew, Thaddeus, Bartholomew, Philip, Thomas, Simeon, Matthew, Mary, Martha, and their brother Lazarus?

Robbie: Yup, the whole gang! They had all gathered together. Was it a special occasion, like a birthday or an anniversary?

Name: Well it was a special moment, but it wasn't a happy occasion. You see the reason Jesus and his friends were together was because they thought it might be the last time they all got together.

Robbie: Why? Was somebody moving?

Name: No, Robbie, no one was moving. Remember, Robbie, some people were angry with Jesus. They didn't like his teaching; they didn't like the way he included everyone, loved everyone. Some people made threats against him; some people wanted him killed. So this was a very special meal; it was a chance for everyone to let Jesus know just how much they loved him, it was a chance for Jesus to let his friends know just how much he loved them.

Robbie: Sometimes, we have special meals together, pancake suppers, hotdog lunch, Advent potluck, Epiphany breakfasts, soup and sandwich, picnics…

Name: That's right, Robbie. Sometimes we share a meal on happy occasions and sometimes we share meals on sad occasions.

Robbie: Like when I was sick and you brought me some soup and we shared it together.

Name: That's right, Robbie, and sometimes when people die, we share a meal together after the service.

Robbie: So we can share our love and care with one another,

Name: That's right, and we also share a special meal in church services sometimes.

Robbie: We do?

Name: Yes we do, Robbie, when we have Communion, we share bread and wine, or grape juice.

Robbie: You call that thimble of grape juice and that cube of bread a meal?

Name: Well, Robbie, it's not a lot to eat or drink but it *does* remind us of the meal Jesus had with his friends, when they were able to share how much they loved him and Jesus was able to share how much he loved them.

Robbie: So it's not so much about the food, it's more about the chance to share the love we have for one another.

Name: That's right, Robbie, and about the chance to remember Jesus and the love he had for us. When we share this meal, we are reminded to share that love with one another.

Robbie: Did you hear that, (Name)?

Name: Hear what?

Robbie: It was my stomach rumbling. I think I'm hungry to share the love I have for everyone and the love I have for Jesus.

Name: Amen, Robbie.

Robbie: Amen.

Lent 6

Palm Sunday

Luke 19:28–40

19:36 As he rode along, people kept spreading their cloaks on the road.

19:38 saying, "Blessed is the king who comes in the name of the Lord! Peace in heaven, and glory in the highest heaven!"

19:39 Some of the Pharisees in the crowd said to him, "Teacher, order your disciples to stop."

Name: Good morning, everyone! Wow, this is an exciting Sunday: Palm Sunday, the last Sunday before Easter. I wonder if Robbie is as excited as I am. Let's call him and find out. 1, 2, 3… *Robbie!*

Name: Good morning, Robbie.

Robbie: Talk about raining on a parade!

Name: What are you talking about, Robbie?

Robbie: I'm talking about the gospel lesson this morning.

Name: Okay, the gospel lesson this morning is about Jesus and his friends coming into the city of Jerusalem.

Robbie: They didn't just stroll in. They paraded in!

Name: They sure did. Jesus was leading the parade. He came into the city riding on a donkey.

Robbie: Or a colt.

Name: And the people, the followers of Jesus, lined the streets and they laid down their coats on the road to make a path.

Robbie: And they shouted, "Hosanna, blessed is the king who comes in the name of the Lord! Peace in heaven, and glory in the highest heaven!"

Name: The people were giving thanks for all the great things Jesus had done.

Robbie: He cared for the sick.

Name: He welcomed the unwelcome.

Robbie: He taught about God's love for all people.

Name: He welcomed children and women.

Robbie: Tax collectors and probably even dragons.

Name: He taught people that they should forgive one another. No wonder people wanted a parade. Jesus had done such wonderful things.

Robbie: So what I don't understand is why some people rained on Jesus' parade. The gospel says, "Some of the Pharisees in the crowd said to him, 'Teacher, order your disciples to stop.'"

Name: Well, Robbie, some people thought Jesus was too disruptive. His teaching, his healing, his compassion and love for all people meant things were going to change, and some people were afraid of change.

Robbie: I know that feeling! There was a time when a dragon wasn't welcome in a church.

Name: But that changed.

Name: There was a time when gay, lesbian, and transgendered people weren't welcome in church.

Robbie: But that changed.

Name: There was a time when women couldn't become ministers.

Robbie: But that changed.

Name: You know, Robbie; in every age God continues to challenge us to change into the people God wants us to be.

Robbie: So even when it rains on our parade we can still shout "Hosanna," as we wait for God's love to rain down upon us.

Name: Let it pour!

Robbie: Amen.

Easter Sunday

John 20:1–18

20:1 Early on the first day of the week, while it was still dark, Mary Magdalene came to the tomb and saw that the stone had been removed from the tomb.

20:2 So she ran and went to Simon Peter and the other disciple, the one whom Jesus loved, and said to them, "They have taken the Lord out of the tomb, and we do not know where they have laid him."

Name: Good morning, everyone. Before you got here this morning I sent Robbie on a mission to find something in his castle. (Pause and look towards or peek inside the castle.)

Name: I'm sure that's where it is, Robbie. Keep looking.

Robbie: Aghh! I wish I was a fire breathing dragon! I can't see a blessed thing in here. Could you pass me a torch… oh wait a minute, (Name). I've got something. Is this what you're looking for?

Name: Not exactly, Robbie, but I think you're getting warmer.

Robbie: Warmer? It's freezing in this cave. Would you fetch me a sweater?

Name: Robbie!

Robbie: Oh all right. Ouch! (Robbie retrieves a crown of thorns) I'm stuck to someone's rosebush.

Name: You're close, Rob, only it's not a rosebush anymore, looks like a crown of thorns. But that's not what I'm looking for. I'm sure it's there. Back you go.

Robbie: Ah, you can't expect me to go back in that cave, after I was accosted by shrubbery.

Name: Please, Rob.

Robbie: All right, but only for you. Aghh it's got me, help! (Robbie returns with a sheet over his head)

Name: Robbie, You're okay, it's just a sheet. Now get back in the cave.

Robbie: Okay but could you give me a clue as to what I'm looking for?

Name: Well, Rob, it has to do with today's lesson. Let me read it to you: (read John 20:1–2)

Early on the first day of the week, while it was still *dark*, Mary Magdalene came to the tomb and saw that the stone had been removed from the tomb. So she ran and went to Simon Peter and the other disciple, the one whom Jesus loved, and said to them, "They have taken the Lord out of the tomb, and we do not know where they have laid him."

Robbie: You want me to find the body of Jesus?

Name: That's right, Rob, the scripture says, "They've taken my master and I don't know what they've done with him."

Robbie: I don't know how to tell you this, but there is no body.

Name: Are you sure?

Robbie: You know, (Name), the scripture reading doesn't end with Jesus' body in the cave.

Name: So there's no body, in that cave.

Robbie: No, but I did find something else.

Name: What's that?

Robbie: Just a minute. (Robbie goes back into the tomb and balloons suddenly appear)

Name: Balloons!

Robbie: You see, (Name), the nails, the crown of thorns, the sheet used to cover the body, all these are left, to remind us that Jesus died. But the balloons are a symbol that reminds us that God's Spirit never dies but lives forever. Balloons are something we see at times of great celebration. And today we celebrate! For Christ has risen and lives in us. Happy Easter, (Name)!

Name: Happy Easter, Robbie. Amen.

2ⁿᵈ Sunday of Easter

John 20:19–31

20:27 Then he said to Thomas, "Put your finger here and see my hands. Reach out your hand and put it in my side. Do not doubt but believe."

Name: Good morning, everyone. Happy Easter! I wonder if Robbie can help us with the gospel this morning? Let's call him. 1, 2, 3…*Robbie!*

Robbie: (Name), can we tell a story together?

Name: I don't see why not, Robbie. Why don't you begin?

Robbie: All right. This is a story about a man named Thomas: "Don't ask so many questions, Thomas." That's what Thomas' teachers said in school.

Name: That's what Thomas' parents said at home.

Robbie: That's what Thomas' friends said.

Name: But Thomas couldn't help it. When the teacher told them things in school, Thomas often asked, "How do you know?"

Robbie: Sometimes that frustrated the teacher. "I know just because I know. It's true because I say so," said the teacher.

Name: But Thomas couldn't stop asking questions. When Thomas grew older, he became one of Jesus' special friends. He became a disciple. Thomas liked Jesus, because Jesus never told him to stop asking questions.

One day Jesus was trying to explain what was going to happen. "I am going away," said Jesus. "I am going to get a place ready for you. God's house has room for you and for everyone else. You know the way to God's house."

Robbie: "No, we don't," said Thomas. "What *is* the way?"

Name: "That's a good question, Thomas," said Jesus. "*I* am the way. If you really love me and love each other, then you *know* the way."

Robbie: "I still don't understand all of it," said Thomas.

Name: "That's okay," said Jesus. "Just keep asking questions."

Robbie: Not long after that, Jesus died. He was killed by people who didn't like the way he said that God loved everyone. Thomas was very sad when Jesus was killed, so when some of the other disciples said Jesus was alive again Thomas really wanted to believe them.

Name: But he just couldn't. His mind kept asking questions: "How can somebody be dead and then be alive again?"

Robbie: Thomas asked, "How can you be sure it was Jesus? How do you know it wasn't somebody else?"

Name: "But we saw him with our own eyes," said the disciples.

Robbie: "Maybe," said Thomas. "But I have to see for myself. I have to see the places in Jesus' hands where they put the nails. Otherwise I won't believe it."

Name: A few days later, Thomas and his friends were together. All the doors were closed, but suddenly, there was Jesus in the room with them. He smiled at Thomas. "Come here, my friend. Touch the places where they put the nails. It really *is* me."

Robbie: Thomas did what Jesus said and was so happy to see Jesus. "Oh, yes, it *is* you Jesus. I am so glad. Now I know that you are alive again. I won't ask any more questions."

Name: "Oh, don't stop asking questions, Thomas," said Jesus. "I am glad you are able to see me so you can be sure. Then you can believe. But there will be lots of people who won't be able to see me. They will ask questions, too. It will be hard for them to believe, just as it was hard for you to believe. I will need you to help tell them my story."

Robbie: "You mean, you're not angry because I didn't believe right away that you were alive again?" Thomas asked.

Name: "No, I'm not angry at all," said Jesus. "I like it when people ask hard questions. But you won't understand everything, Thomas. You will never find answers to *all* your questions. Just remember that I love you and that God loves you. Nobody can prove that part, but it is the part that is the most true."

Robbie: Amen.

3rd Sunday of Easter

John 21:1–19

21:12 Jesus said to them, "Come and have breakfast." Now none of the disciples dared to ask him, "Who are you?" because they knew it was the Lord.

21:15 When they had finished breakfast, Jesus said to Simon Peter, "Simon son of John, do you love me more than these?" He said to him, "Yes, Lord; you know that I love you." Jesus said to him, "Feed my lambs."

Name: Good morning everyone, Happy Easter 3! I sure am looking forward to a visit from Robbie this morning. Let's call him. 1, 2, 3…*Robbie!*

Name: Good morning, Robbie.

Robbie: I could order the pancakes, or I could have eggs and bacon, or I could order am omelet with…

Name: Robbie, what are you talking about?

Robbie: I'm talking about the gospel lesson this morning.

Name: The gospel lesson?

Robbie: In the gospel lesson this morning, Jesus appears to his friends for a third time and invites them to have breakfast, so I just want to make sure I'm prepared with my breakfast order.

Name: Oh, Robbie, I don't think Jesus was taking breakfast orders. I think he was inviting the disciples to feed others.

Robbie: Feed *others?* But I haven't had my breakfast yet. How can I feed others?

Name: Well, Robbie, I think Jesus has already fed you?

Robbie: I don't *think* so! My tummy is still grumbling.

Name: Robbie, do you remember when you were a lonely dragon?

Robbie: I do. It was before you invited me to be part of the (community name).

Name: So because you were invited to (community name), your loneliness was fed?

Robbie: That's true; I was hungry for a caring community.

Name: And do you remember when you didn't have place to live?

Robbie: I do, and you invited me to live in the castle.

Name: And you were fed with shelter and kindness. And do you remember when you were hungry to be accepted and loved?

Robbie: I do, and you accepted and loved me.

Name: Do you know what the word breakfast means?

Robbie: Hash browns?

Name: No.

Robbie: Golden toast with raspberry…?

Name: No, Robbie. The word breakfast means "to break fast."

Robbie: But I'm not even old enough to drive!

Name: Not brake fast, but *break* fast. Fasting is when we don't have something. For example, when we wake up in the morning we haven't eaten all night. That's like fasting. In the morning we break that fast by eating something.

Robbie: Breakfast.

Name: That's right. In the morning we break our night of fasting. But we also fast from other things.

Robbie: Like…

Name: Acceptance.

Robbie: Love.

Name: Justice.

Robbie: Forgiveness.

Name: So Jesus was breaking the fast of the disciples. By showing himself to them. Jesus encouraged the disciples to break the fasts of other people – of loneliness, or fear, or sadness – by feeding them with love, acceptance, and hope.

Robbie: Sounds like breaking fast is the best meal of the day!

Name: Amen.

4th Sunday of Easter

John 10:22–30

10:27 My sheep hear my voice. I know them, and they follow me.

10:28 I give them eternal life, and they will never perish. No one will snatch them out of my hand.

Name: Good morning, everyone. It's great to be here today. I'm looking forward to chatting with Robbie about today's lesson. Let's call him 1, 2, 3… *Robbie!*

Robbie: (singing) When I'm calling you, ooo, ooo.

Name: Wow, Robbie, what's got into you this morning?

Robbie: The gospel lesson that's what.

Name: I don't remember any singing in today's lesson.

Robbie: No singing, but there's a whole lot of calling.

Name: Oh I understand, Robbie. In today's lesson people have gathered around Jesus and want to know if he's the Messiah.

Robbie: The suspense was killing them!

Name: But I don't understand. Jesus has already shown them who he is.

Robbie: That's right. He's healed the sick, he's welcomed the stranger, and he's shown love to the unlovable. He's called for justice for all God's people.

Name: But people still wanted Jesus to say he was the Messiah.

Robbie: Some people thought the Messiah was going to kick the Romans out of Israel. Some people thought the Messiah was going to be an earthly king like King David.

Name: But Jesus wasn't that kind of Messiah. He was a Messiah that wanted God's Kindom of love, of justice, of compassion, and care for one another to come on earth, just like we imagine it is in heaven.

Robbie: But the people just couldn't hear him.

Name: Sometimes people don't hear because they don't really want to listen.

Robbie: Like when my dad asks me to take out the trash, sometimes I pretend I just don't hear him because I don't want to take out the trash; or when my mother says it's bath time, or time for bed. I just can't seem to hear her.

Name: Well, maybe that's the problem in today's gospel; the people who ask Jesus if he's the Messiah don't really want to hear what Jesus says.

Robbie: But Jesus keeps calling, hoping that we will hear his voice, that we will come and follow him and his example so that we can have full lives of goodness, love, peace, and hope!

Name: That's something I think we *all* need to hear.

Robbie: What?

Name: I said…

Robbie: Just kidding, (Name). I heard you the first time.

Name: Amen.

5th Sunday of Easter

John 13:31–35

13:34 "I give you a new commandment, that you love one another. Just as I have loved you, you also should love one another.

13:35 By this everyone will know that you are my disciples, if you have love for one another."

Name: Good morning, everyone. I'm sure looking forward to visiting with Robbie this morning. Let's call him. 1, 2, 3... *Robbie!*

Name: Good morning, Robbie!

Robbie: Good morning, (Name). Well, my bags were packed, I was all ready, and then I was told I couldn't go!

Name: Where were you going to go, Robbie?

Robbie: Well, I was ready to go with my best friend who was moving to a new city.

Name: Oh, Robbie, I'm sorry to hear your friend is moving, but if you moved then we'd miss you.

Robbie: *Oh,* I didn't think of that. So now I'm *really* upset. I want to be with my best friend but I don't want to leave (church).

Name: It is hard isn't, Robbie? I'm sure you're going to miss your friend.

Robbie: I sure am! My friend was the best! We'd laugh together and I could tell her my secrets; she helped me when I felt sad. I really loved her!

Name: You know, Robbie, I think that's how the disciples felt.

Robbie: Really?

Name: Really, Robbie. In the gospel lesson this morning, Jesus tells his friends that he has to leave them.

Robbie: That must have been really sad for Jesus' friends. Jesus was a friend who loved the disciples.

Name: Not just the disciples. Jesus loved *all* people. He loved the sick, he loved children, and he loved woman and men, rich and poor.

Robbie: So if Jesus was leaving, who was going to love all the people?

Name: Well, Robbie, Jesus didn't leave without giving us something.

Robbie: Was it his collection of fishing nets?

Name: No.

Robbie: His sandals?

Name: No.

Robbie: Well, (Name), Jesus didn't *have* much. What could he leave us?

Name: Robbie, Jesus left us with a *commandment*.

Robbie: A *commandment*. Sounds kind of big. Will it fit in my castle?

Name: A commandment isn't a *thing*, it's an instruction.

Robbie: And Jesus left a commandment for us?

Name: Yes, Robbie, he did. Jesus said to his friends, "I give you a new commandment, that you love one another. Just as I have loved you, you also should love one another. By this everyone will know that you are my disciples, if you have love for one another."

Robbie: So even though Jesus was leaving, he left with us with a commandment to follow and if we follow it he will still be with us?

Name: That's right, Robbie. Jesus told his friends that just because he couldn't stay with them they shouldn't stop loving, because the best thing Jesus gave was love. I'm sure your friend hopes that you won't stop loving her?

Robbie: I won't.

Name: And maybe the best way to show your love to your friend is to continue to love others.

Robbie: I think that's the best going-away present I could give.

Name: Amen.

6ᵗʰ Sunday of Easter

John 14:23–29

14:23 Jesus answered him, "Those who love me will keep my word, and [God] will love them, and we will come to them and make our home with them.

14:24 Whoever does not love me does not keep my words; and the word that you hear is not mine, but is from [God] who sent me.

14:25 "I have said these things to you while I am still with you.

14:26 But the Advocate, the Holy Spirit, whom [God] will send in my name, will teach you everything, and remind you of all that I have said to you."

Name: (Adapt as necessary if the Easter season this year includes seven Sundays.) Good morning, everyone. Can you believe it? It's the last Sunday of the Easter Season. I wonder how Robbie is this morning? Let's find out. 1, 2, 3… *Robbie!*

Name: Good morning, Robbie. Can you believe it's the last week of the Easter season?

Robbie: I know. I'm a little worried I'll start to forget.

Name: Forget what?

Robbie: See that's what I *mean!* Even *you* are starting to forget!

Name: What?

Robbie: Jesus! How am I supposed to remember if someone as smart as you can't remember?

Name: Oh, Robbie, I'm not going to forget Jesus and you won't forget either.

Robbie: What? Are you going to call me up every morning and say, "Hey, Robbie, don't forget Jesus."

Name: Robbie…

Robbie: Are you going to pop up in my math class and say, "Hey, Robbie, don't forget Jesus?"

Name: Robbie…

Robbie: Are you going to text me all the time and remind me not to forget Jesus?

Name: *Robbie!* I may remind you sometimes and maybe sometimes you'll remind *me* about all the wonderful things Jesus said and did. But Jesus told the disciples that God would send a gift to them that would help them remember.

Robbie: A gift? Maybe Jesus has a Facebook page and I could get notifications every day? Or maybe just a tweet if Jesus is really busy. Or how about once a month a member of the choir comes to my house and gives me a singing telegram telling me to remember Jesus. Or…

Name: Robbie, stop.

Robbie: Sorry, it's just I get excited about gifts.

Name: Robbie, the gift Jesus said God would give us is the Holy Spirit.

Robbie: Okay…so where *is* this "Holy Spirit"?

Name: Well, Robbie, I think the Holy Spirit is everywhere people are loving each other.

Robbie: Those were Jesus' words!

Name: I think the Holy Spirit is everywhere people are seeking justice and being compassionate.

Robbie: Those were Jesus' words, too.

Name: That's what Jesus told his friends; he said whoever keeps my word loves me and I will be with them.

Robbie: So, even though Easter is over, the gift of the Holy Spirit will remind us of Jesus' words. Every time we're loving, forgiving, or peace-making, Jesus is alive in our hearts and in the world.

Name: I think that's it.

Robbie: (Name), you know, I still think it's not a bad idea for the choir to show up with a singing telegram about Jesus just to make sure we don't forget.

Name: I'll pass that on to the choir. Amen.

Robbie: Amen.

Ascension of the Lord

(7th Sunday of Easter)

John 17:20–26

17:23 I in them and you in me, that they may become completely one, so that the world may know that you have sent me and have loved them even as you have loved me.

Name: Good morning, everyone. Wow, the last Sunday of the Easter season! It's gone by so fast. I wonder what's next. Maybe Robbie can tell us? Let's call him. 1, 2, 3… *Robbie!*

Name: Good morning, Robbie.

Robbie: *Hey*, I know you!

Name: Well, I should *hope* so!

Robbie: No, I mean I really *know* you!

Name: Okay, Robbie, how do you really know me?

Robbie: Well, the first thing is, I know the sound of your voice.

Name: Okay, but how *else* do you know me?

Robbie: Well, I know your favourite colour, I know your favourite food, I know your favourite subject in school, I know you are afraid of spiders, I know who your friends are, I know where you live, I know your favourite type of music, I know…

Name: Okay, okay, I get it, Robbie. You know me, but how do you *really know* me?

Robbie: Well, I guess I really know you by your love.

Name: By my love?

Robbie: That's how Jesus' disciples knew him even after he died.

Name: By his love?

Robbie: That's right. In the gospel lesson this morning, Jesus prays for his friends.

Name: That's right. He says, "I made your name known to them, and I will make it known, so that the love with which you have loved me may be in them, and I in them."

Robbie: So that's how we know God.

Name: We know God by seeing God's love in the beauty of the world.

Robbie: In the love we feel in music, art, and drama.

Name: And especially in the love we have for one another.

Robbie: So love is the one thing!

Name: It's the one thing that holds us together. It's the one thing that Jesus came to show us.

Robbie: So, (Name), "one" isn't *really* the loneliest number...

Name: Not when we're all together, when we're *one in love*.

Robbie: Well, I'm praying that we all know each other by our love.

Name: Well, I know you, Robbie, and I know you're all about the love.

Robbie: Amen.

Name: Amen.

Pentecost Sunday

Acts 2:1–21

2:1 When the day of Pentecost had come, they were all together in one place.

2:2 And suddenly from heaven there came a sound like the rush of a violent wind, and it filled the entire house where they were sitting.

2:3 Divided tongues, as of fire, appeared among them, and a tongue rested on each of them.

2:4 All of them were filled with the Holy Spirit and began to speak in other languages, as the Spirit gave them ability.

Name: Good morning, everyone! And Happy Pentecost Sunday! I'm sure Robbie is excited to share his Pentecost Spirit, so let's call him. 1, 2 , 3… *Robbie!*

Name: Good morning, Robbie.

Robbie: (Spanish) *Hola*, (Name), *¿Cómo estás?*

Name: Uh, sorry, Robbie. I don't understand Spanish.

Robbie: *Comment ça va?*

Name: Is that French?

Robbie: *Sahwahdee kap?*

Name: Thai?

Robbie: *Guten Tag?*

Name: German?

Robbie: *Ann yeong hasey o?*

Name: Korean?

Robbie: Aghh, I give up.

Name: English. *Right?*

Robbie: It's no use.

Name: What's no use?

Robbie: Well, I was hoping that what happened in today's lesson would happen to me.

Name: What's that?

Robbie: Today's lesson is all about what happened on the first Pentecost.

Name: That's right, the passage from Acts says, "When the day of Pentecost had come, they were all together in one place. And suddenly from heaven there came a sound like the rush of a violent wind, and it filled the entire house where they were sitting."

Robbie: And then, "Divided tongues, as of fire, appeared among them, and a tongue rested on each of them. All of them were filled with the Holy Spirit and began to speak in other languages, as the Spirit gave them ability." I thought I might have an advantage with the whole language thing.

Name: How's that?

Robbie: Well first of all, have a look at my tongue.

Name: Robbie, I'm not sure…

Robbie: No, go ahead, really. See, it's divided.

Name: Oh I see what you mean, Robbie.

Robbie: And I'm a dragon right?

Name: Right.

Robbie: And dragons breathe…

Name: Fire!

Robbie: Exactly! So I thought this morning's lesson would be a snap. "Divided tongues, like fire," resting on them. I thought I'd be able to speak so everyone could understand me.

Name: Well, Robbie, learning a new language can be hard work and take a lot of time, but we can talk to one another in other ways.

Robbie: How?

Name: Well, when I see your smile, you're communicating friendliness.

Robbie: And when I'm frowning?

Name: You're telling me that you're upset or something's bothering you.

Robbie: When I'm laughing…

Name: You're communicating joy. What do you think the friends of Jesus wanted to tell others?

Robbie: I think they wanted to tell others about God's love for everyone.

Name: The kind of love that Jesus communicated to his friends. You know, Robbie, God still gives us the ability to speak to others, even when we don't know the words.

Robbie: Through our caring for one another…

Name: You're speaking the language of love.

Robbie: When we hold hands with someone who's sad or lonely…

Name: You're speaking the language of love.

Robbie: When we stand up for someone who is being bullied or left out…

Name: That's the language of love. That's the language the friends of Jesus were learning on that first Pentecost.

Robbie: And that's the language we're still learning today.

Name: Amen.

Robbie: *Hasta luego*, Baby.

Trinity Sunday

John 16:12–15

16:12 "I still have many things to say to you, but you cannot bear them now.

16:13 When the Spirit of truth comes, he will guide you into all the truth; for he will not speak on his own, but will speak whatever he hears, and he will declare to you the things that are to come."

Name: Good morning, everyone. To tell you the truth, I'm a little worried about Robbie; he's been acting kind of strange. Let's call and see what's up. 1, 2, 3… *Robbie!*

Robbie: I can't bear it!

Name: Can't bear what?

Robbie: The truth!

Name: The truth.

Robbie: That's right, the truth. Last week Carrot…

Name: Carrot is your goldfish.

Robbie: That's right. Last week Carrot was swimming in her bowl, happy and swimmy as usual. Then last night when I went to feed her, she was just floating at the top of her bowl. I thought she was just resting.

Name: Oh, Robbie, I hate to tell you…

Robbie: Don't tell me! I can't bear it.

Name: You know, Robbie, your story reminds me of the gospel lesson this morning.

Robbie: Did Jesus know about floating goldfish?

Name: I'm not sure about that, Robbie. But Jesus *did* know that sometimes we find out things that seem too hard to bear. In today's reading, Jesus has to tell his friends that he wouldn't be with them much longer.

Robbie: (singing) La, la, la, la, I can't *hear* you!

Name: Well, that may have been how the disciples of Jesus felt. They couldn't bear the thought that Jesus would leave them.

Robbie: I think I know how they felt.

Name: Jesus knew, too. But he told his friends, "even after I die, I will make sure you are not alone."

Robbie: How did he make sure of that?

Name: Well, Jesus said that after he left them the Spirit of truth would come and help them.

Robbie: The Spirit of truth? What's that?

Name: Robbie, the Spirit is the presence of God sent to help and guide us in our lives.

Robbie: Like when the truth is too hard to hear?

Name: That's right. Remember when Jesus died?

Robbie: The friends of Jesus couldn't bear it!

Name: But they *did* bear it, because God's spirit came to them. The Spirit helped them share their sadness with one another when they comforted one another, when they shared all the stories they had of when Jesus was with them. The times he healed them, the times he loved them, all the things Jesus taught them about God's love. And the Spirit was with them and helped them to bear the sadness.

Robbie: The Spirit helped them.

Name: And the Spirit will help you, too, Robbie.

Robbie: You know, (Name), I think I know the truth about my goldfish Carrot. And I think I can bear the truth that she's gone, because the Spirit of God's love is in you and my friends and I'm not alone.

Name: That's the Spirit of God's love at work.

Robbie: In you.

Name: In you.

Robbie: In each of us. Amen.

Name: Amen.

Proper 4 [9]

Sunday between May 29 and June 4 inclusive

Luke 7:1–10, MSG

7:6–8 Jesus went with them. When he was still quite far from the house, the captain sent friends to tell him, "Master, you don't have to go to all this trouble. I'm not that good a person, you know. I'd be embarrassed for you to come to my house, even embarrassed to come to you in person. Just give the order and my servant will get well."

Name: Good morning, everyone. I wonder how Robbie is doing this week. Let's call him. 1, 2, 3… *Robbie!*

Robbie: Is there a doctor in the house? Is there a doctor?

Name: Oh no! Robbie, what's the matter? Why do you need a doctor?

Robbie: It's not me, (Name), it's the servant in the gospel lesson this morning. He's so sick he might die!

Name: That *is* serious but, Robbie, you do know the gospel lesson was written thousands of years ago?

Robbie: So we're too late?

Name: For the sick servant in the gospel this morning, yes. But not for us.

Robbie: Why is it not too late for us?

Name: Well, Robbie, do you remember the time you were sick and you thought it would be too much bother for me to come and visit you?

Robbie: I do. I remember thinking that you were far too busy with important things to come and see me. So I told you not to bother.

Name: That sounds just like the man in the story this morning. He didn't think he was worthy enough to have Jesus come to his house and visit his sick friend.

Robbie: But Jesus didn't think he was so important that he couldn't visit the man and his sick friend.

Name: That's right. Jesus was willing to come and visit. In fact, he was on his way to the man's house, when he got the message not to come.

Robbie: The Roman soldier was so grateful that Jesus would stop what he was doing and come to see his friend, the servant.

Name: How did you feel when I told you I was going to come and visit you, that I wasn't too busy.

Robbie: Well, I actually started to feel a bit better.

Name: Why do you think you started to feel better?

Robbie: I guess I started to feel better because I didn't feel so alone.

Name: Sometimes when we're sick, it's not just our bodies that are unwell, but sometimes our hearts are aching because we feel alone in our sickness.

Robbie: And sometimes, the best medicine is the medicine of friendship and caring.

Name: That's what I think helped the man and his servant in today's story.

Robbie: Even though Jesus didn't see the servant…

Name: His message of care and love got through. It got through to the Roman soldier, who was caring for his servant.

Robbie: And he felt better.

Name: And that message of love and care Jesus showed the Roman soldier, who didn't think he deserved Jesus' attention, was passed on from *him* to the sick servant.

Robbie: And we're told *he* got better.

Name: Love and care are powerful medicines.

Robbie: So I guess when we come together there are lots of doctors of love and care in the house.

Name: There sure are.

Robbie: Send in the next patient!

Name: Amen.

Proper 5 [10]

Sunday between June 5 and June 11 inclusive

Luke 7:11–17

7:11–13a Not long after that, Jesus went to the village Nain. His disciples were with him, along with quite a large crowd. As they approached the village gate, they met a funeral procession – a woman's only son was being carried out for burial. And the mother was a widow. When Jesus saw her, his heart broke.

Name: Good morning, everyone! I'm really looking forward to talking with Robbie this morning and I hope you are too. Let's call him out of the castle. 1, 2, 3… *Robbie!*

Name: Good morning, Robbie.

Robbie: Good morning.

Name: Well, Robbie, I'm so glad you're here today because…

Robbie: Excuse me, but I want to…

Name: Not now, Robbie, we've got a lot to talk about this morning, the gospel lesson is really…

Robbie: But I really need to tell you…

Name: Not now, Robbie, we've got to stick to the script! We've got a whole worship service to get through: hymns to sing, offering to be collected, sermon to hear, prayers to read…!

Robbie: Exactly, Jesus…

Name: Robbie, you'll have to stop interrupting me otherwise we'll be over time and you know how people like to finish the service according to the schedule. Now, in the gospel lesson this morning Jesus…

Robbie: That's my point!

Name: What's your point, Robbie!

Robbie: My point is that Jesus is a major interrupterer!

Name: Major interrupterer? Is interrupterer a word?

Robbie: Well it should be, because Jesus is the king of interrupters. In the gospel lesson this morning, Jesus and his friends were visiting a village called Nain.

Name: And when they got to the village gate, they met a funeral procession. A funeral procession is the when people follow the body of someone who has died to the cemetery.

Robbie: In the funeral procession that Jesus saw, a woman was walking behind her only son, who had died, and they were carrying his body to the cemetery. The mother had to bury her son; she had no husband and no other children.

Name: When Jesus saw the woman…

Robbie: His heart broke.

Name: And…

Robbie: And he interrupted the whole funeral procession.

Name: Jesus was so moved with compassion for the woman that he interrupted the funeral so that he could offer her his care and concern, he wanted to let her know she wasn't alone.

Robbie: Jesus is a good interrupterer!

Name: You're right, Robbie. Jesus often interrupts us in order to remind us of what's most important in our lives.

Robbie: Like interrupting…

Name: So that we can care for one another.

Robbie: Exactly! Amen.

Proper 6 [11]

Sunday between June 12 and June 18 inclusive

Luke 7:36 – 8:3, MSG

7:36–39 One of the Pharisees asked him over for a meal. He went to the Pharisee's house and sat down at the dinner table. Just then a woman of the village, the town harlot, having learned that Jesus was a guest in the home of the Pharisee, came with a bottle of very expensive perfume and stood at his feet, weeping, raining tears on his feet. Letting down her hair, she dried his feet, kissed them, and anointed them with the perfume. When the Pharisee who had invited him saw this, he said to himself, "If this man was the prophet I thought he was, he would have known what kind of woman this is who is falling all over him."

Name: Good morning, everyone. I' am so glad to be in church this morning! Aren't you? Hmmm, that didn't sound very glad. I wonder if Robbie is glad to be here today. Let's call him out and find out. 1, 2, 3… *Robbie!*

Name: Good morning, Robbie.

Robbie: Good morning.

Name: You know, Robbie, I asked everyone if they were glad to be in church this morning and I was wondering, "are *you* glad to be in church this morning?"

Robbie: S'alright.

Name: *S'alright?* That doesn't sound very glad, Robbie.

Robbie: Well I mean, sure, I'm glad to be in church this morning; I get to see my friends, I get to sing, and I get to pray. You know, "s'alright."

Name: You know, Robbie, I think that's how the people who invited Jesus to dinner felt. If the people were asked how they felt about Jesus coming to dinner, they might have said…

Robbie: S'alright.

Name: But when a woman who wasn't invited to the supper heard that Jesus was in town, she showed up. And she was so glad to see Jesus that she even started to *cry!* She washed his feet with expensive, perfumed soap, and when she didn't have a towel to dry them, she used her *hair!* The host of the dinner was…

Robbie: Bothered! Really bothered! He was so bothered he said to everyone, "Well, if this is the kind of people Jesus meets with, I don't think so much of him."

Name: But then Jesus said to everyone, "You know, when I came to your house, you didn't say hello, you didn't take my coat, you've acted like you don't care!"

Robbie: And then he said to everyone, "But *this* woman, who is not even the host of the party – she had to *crash* the party, wasn't even on the list of invited guests – *she's* shown more care to me than all of you put together.

Name: She knows how to make someone feel at home!

Robbie: She's a hostess with the *mostess!*

Name: Preach it, brother Robbie!

Robbie: She's showing us that as followers of Jesus were called not to be just…

Name: S'alright…

Robbie: Jesus is calling us to be *dynamite!*

Name: To blow off the doors of ingratitude.

Robbie: Be the *gratitude with attitude!*

Name: Just like the woman.

Robbie: Word!

Name: Word!

Proper 7 [12]

Sunday between June 19 and June 25 inclusive

Luke 8:26–39

8:26 Then they arrived at the country of the Gerasenes, which is opposite Galilee.

8:27 As he stepped out on land, a man of the city who had demons met him. For a long time he had worn no clothes, and he did not live in a house but in the tombs.

8:28 When he saw Jesus, he fell down before him and shouted at the top of his voice, "What have you to do with me, Jesus, Son of the Most High God? I beg you, do not torment me."

Name: Good morning, everyone. I'm sure glad to be here this morning and I'm really looking forward to seeing Robbie. Let's call him. 1, 2, 3… *Robbie!*

Name: Good morning, Robbie.

Robbie: What in the world possessed you?

Name: What do you mean?

Robbie: I mean, what possessed you to read the gospel lesson for this morning? Did you listen to the reading? Spooky. Demons and graveyards… I thought I took a wrong turn and ended up in a scary movie.

Name: I see what you mean, Robbie, and I have to admit the reading this morning was kind of scary. But did you notice what Jesus did in that story?

Robbie: I sure did and I wasn't sure who was more crazy – the man who was shouting and acting strange, or Jesus for not getting back on the boat and sailing away.

Name: You know, Robbie, sometimes we are afraid of people who act differently. Where I shop, there is a man who I sometimes see and he shouts out things, sometimes not very nice things.

Robbie: Kind of like the man in the story today. So what happened? Did the store manager kick him out?

Name: Actually, Robbie, one day I asked the store manager about the man, and he told me he had a disease, a sickness, that made him shout and that I didn't have to be afraid of him.

Robbie: So what did you do? Shop somewhere else?

Name: No, Robbie. Now when I see the man in the grocery store, I say hello, and sometimes he says hello back. Some days he still shouts, but I'm not afraid anymore. And you know what, Robbie, I think the man appreciates that I say hello.

Robbie: Wow, where did you get the courage to not run away?

Name: Actually, Robbie, I got the courage from Jesus.

Robbie: From Jesus?

Name: That's right. In the gospel this morning, we heard about a man.

Robbie: A man who shouted and acted strange.

Name: A man who had to live in the cemetery because people chased him from everywhere else in the town, even tried to lock him up. But Jesus didn't run away. He went right up to the man and talked to him just like he would with anyone.

Robbie: And he tried to help him.

Name: He did, Robbie, he knew that the man was sick, but that was no reason not to love him.

Robbie: Like when I'm sick, my parents love me even more.

Name: Exactly, Robbie. Sometimes we get a cold or a broken bone, but sometimes people get a sickness in their heads and they need love and compassion even more.

Robbie: So this isn't really a scary story *after all*. It's *really* a story about learning to love people who are hard to understand and who seem different.

Name: Robbie, I think you've got it! Amen.

Proper 8 [13]

Sunday between June 26 and July 2 inclusive

Luke 9:51–62, MSG

9:59–61 Jesus said to another, "Follow me."

He said, "Certainly, but first excuse me for a couple of days, please. I have to make arrangements for my father's funeral."

Jesus refused. "First things first. Your business is life, not death. And life is urgent: Announce God's kingdom!"

Then another said, "I'm ready to follow you, Master, but first excuse me while I get things straightened out at home."

Jesus said, "No procrastination. No backward looks. You can't put God's kingdom off till tomorrow. Seize the day."

Name: Good morning, everyone. I wonder if Robbie is ready to have a visit with us this morning? Let's call him and see if he's home. 1, 2, 3,... *Robbie!*

Name: Good morning, Robbie.

Robbie: Excuse me?

Name: I said,...

Robbie: Excuse me?

Name: Robbie, is there something wrong with your hearing this morning? I said...

Robbie: No, no, no, (Name), I heard you loud and clear. It's just that "excuse me" is what the man asked Jesus to do for him.

Name: Oh, I see. You're talking about the gospel lesson for this morning.

Robbie: That's right! In the gospel lesson, Jesus is on his way to the city of Jerusalem.

Name: It was not a trip he wanted to make. He knew that there were people in Jerusalem who wanted to do him harm.

Robbie: So why didn't he just say he was too busy, or that he had a doctor's appointment that day, or that his donkey had a flat and was in the shop?

Name: Well, Robbie, those would have been lame excuses! And Jesus knew that if you wanted to follow God's path, you couldn't make excuses.

Robbie: Wow, it reminds me of the time I didn't get my homework done.

Name: Did you have a good excuse?

Robbie: I *thought* it was a good excuse; I was having such a good time playing with my friends that I didn't do it.

Name: And did your teacher think it was a good excuse?

Robbie: Not so much.

Name: In the gospel story, people said they wanted to follow Jesus, but when it got uncomfortable they made excuses not to carry on.

Robbie: Like I wanted to do well in school, but when it got hard I made excuses not to do the homework.

Name: Exactly.

Robbie: My teacher told me that sometimes learning will be difficult.

Name: Just like Jesus told those who followed him that it wouldn't always be easy to be a disciple.

Robbie: Sometimes people will be upset that you choose to care for people who others don't care about.

Name: Sometimes, you may feel that speaking up for people who are being hurt or bullied could get you in trouble. But Jesus tells us…

Robbie: That's no excuse.

Name: Jesus said to those who wanted to follow in his way, "No procrastination. No backward looks. You can't put God's kindom off until tomorrow. Seize the day."

Robbie: You know, I'm glad we're on this journey together. It helps to keep us on the right track.

Name: Excuse me?

Robbie: I said…

Name: I heard what you said. It's just that our time is up and we need to move along in the service.

Robbie: Well, *excuse* me! Amen.

Name: Amen.

Proper 9 [14]

Sunday between July 3 and July 9 inclusive

Luke 10:1–11, 16–20

10:1 After this the Lord appointed seventy others and sent them on ahead of him in pairs to every town and place where he himself intended to go.

10:2 He said to them, "The harvest is plentiful, but the laborers are few; therefore ask the Lord of the harvest to send out laborers into his harvest.

10:3 Go on your way. See, I am sending you out like lambs into the midst of wolves.

10:4 Carry no purse, no bag, no sandals; and greet no one on the road.

10:5 Whatever house you enter, first say, 'Peace to this house'!"

Name: Good morning, everyone! It's great to be here this morning. Now that school is out, I wonder what Robbie's plans are? Let's find out. 1, 2, 3... *Robbie!*

Name: Good morning, Robbie.

Robbie: (Robbie comes out with a full backpack) Good morning, (Name).

Name: Wow, Robbie, you certainly have a full backpack. Are you going camping?

Robbie: I'm going on a road trip! And I'm trying to pack everything I'll need.

Name: What have you packed?

Robbie: Well, I've got my scuba gear, I've got my long pants, my short pants, my blender, my stove, my rubber boots, my winter boots, my computer, my pots and pans, my pajamas, my bicycle, my scooter...

Name: Whoa, Robbie, hold on. It sounds like you're trying to take everything on your trip.

Robbie: That's what my mom said. She told me I could only take one bag. How am I going to take everything in one bag?

Name: You know, Robbie, I think the gospel lesson this morning could help you pack.

Robbie: I don't think so, (Name); my mom said I have to do it myself.

Name: No, Robbie, what I mean is, the gospel lesson has some good advice about what we *really* need to pack when we go on a trip.

Robbie: Okay, let's hear it.

Name: Well, in today's gospel lesson Jesus is sending out 70 new disciples.

Robbie: Seventy! All crammed onto one little donkey?

Name: No, Robbie, there is no donkey. It's a walking trip.

Robbie: Wow, I guess they'd have to carry heavy backpacks.

Name: Actually, Robbie, Jesus told the new disciples not to carry *any* bags.

Robbie: Where will they keep their clothes and their shoes and their espresso machine?

Name: They won't take any shoes or extra clothes. They won't pack any food or bring any money.

Robbie: Uh, (Name)? Are you sure you've got the right lesson, because if Jesus told his disciples not to pack any clothes, or food, or money, what did Jesus tell his disciples to bring with them?

Name: Just one thing. Can you guess what that was?

Robbie: A Swiss Army knife. You know the kind with a screwdriver, bottle opener, scissors, toothpick…

Name: No, Robbie, not a Swiss Army knife. Just one thing, and that one thing was *peace*.

Robbie: Well, I don't think there will be much peace on my trip if I don't bring a change of socks and underwear!

Name: The trip the disciples were going on was a trip to tell people about God's love and that God's peaceable kindom was open to all people.

Robbie: And when the disciples shared this message of God's love and peace to people on their trip, they trusted that God would open people's hearts and their homes, and that people would welcome the disciples into their homes and offer them food and shelter.

Name: That's right.

Robbie: You know, (Name), I probably don't need to take so much stuff on my trip. It will just weigh me down and I'll be grumpy with my family and friends and I'll worry the whole time that I forgot something.

Name: That's why Jesus told his friends to take with them only what was essential.

Robbie: Peace.

Name: And love.

Robbie: And maybe my toothbrush.

Name: Amen.

Proper 10 [15]

Sunday between July 10 and July 16 inclusive

Luke 10:25–37

10:25 Just then a lawyer stood up to test Jesus. "Teacher," he said, "what must I do to inherit eternal life?"

10:27 [The lawyer] answered, "You shall love the Lord your God with all your heart, and with all your soul, and with all your strength, and with all your mind; and your neighbor as yourself."

10:28 And [Jesus] said to him, "You have given the right answer; do this, and you will live."

Name: Good morning, everyone. I wonder how Robbie is doing this morning. Let's call him out and see. 1, 2, 3... *Robbie!*

Name: Good morning, Robbie.

Robbie: Good morning, (Name)! I'm glad to see you weathered the storm last night. You know, the storm kind of reminds me of the gospel lesson this morning.

Name: Really, Robbie? I don't remember any storm in the reading this morning? The reading wasn't the story of Jesus calming the storm when he and his friends were in a boat crossing the sea?

Robbie: No, (Name), not that storm.

Name: Well, Robbie, I don't remember any other storm that Jesus calmed.

Robbie: Well, there are different kinds of storms.

Name: Like what?

Robbie: Well, one time I didn't get my homework done and my teacher... I thought he was going to blow his top!

Name: Oh, I've seen *that* kind of storm!

Robbie: Me too! Today in the gospel lesson Jesus was really creating a storm.

Name: How was he doing that, Robbie?

Robbie: Well, (Name), you know how Jesus spent his time teaching people about God's Kindom.

Name: I remember Jesus was teaching people to care for one another.

Robbie: And...

Name: And Jesus was teaching us that when we love one another we love God.

Robbie: That's what I'm talking about. Jesus was creating a storm!

Name: How, Robbie?

Robbie: Well, (Name), when Jesus was teaching he wasn't just teaching his friends, he was teaching everyone who would hear.

Name: He was teaching the Jewish people, and the Gentiles, and the Samaritans, and all the other people.

Robbie: But in the gospel lesson this morning some people questioned his teaching.

Name: One person, a lawyer, a teacher of the law, asked Jesus a question.

Robbie: Yes, and that *would* be tricky; lawyers know a lot of rules and laws.

Name: That's right, Robbie, and the Jewish people had over 600 laws they had to obey. Can you imagine trying to remember all those rules?

Robbie: I can barely remember the rule to wash my hands before I eat!

Name: Trying to remember over 600 laws was very hard to do. And each law was just as important as all the other ones. So the lawyer tried to trick Jesus by asking him which of the laws was the most important.

Robbie: Yes, and that's where the storm comes in. Jesus said the most important law was to love God with all your heart and soul and mind…

Name: And?

Robbie: And love your neighbour as yourself.

Name: So Jesus rolled all the laws into one law.

Robbie: He sure did, and it caused quite a storm. It blew the lawyer away!

Name: So as a follower of Jesus, loving God and our neighbour and ourselves is the law we're trying to follow now. Every year, our national church donates money to relief work that is being carried out by our global church partners and relief workers in countries that are suffering because of storms.

Robbie: That's loving our neighbour as ourselves.

Name: That's sharing God's love.

Robbie: Well, (Name), I rest my case!

Name: Lesson adjourned! Amen.

Proper 11 [16]

Sunday between July 17 and July 23

Luke 10:38–42

10:40 But Martha was distracted by her many tasks; so she came to him and asked, "Lord, do you not care that my sister has left me to do all the work by myself? Tell her then to help me."

10:41 But the Lord answered her, "Martha, Martha, you are worried and distracted by many things";

Name: Good morning, everyone! I hope everyone has been enjoying the summer. I wonder how Robbie was this week? Let's call him. 1, 2, 3... *Robbie!*

Name: Good morning, Robbie.

Robbie: (talking to himself) Name tags; don't forget 100 name tags, plates, knives and forks, make macaroni salad for 100 dragons...

Name: Robbie, snap out of it!

Robbie: Huh? Oh sorry, (Name), I didn't hear what you said.

Name: I said, good morning, Robbie.

Robbie: Oh yeah, good morning, uh...

Name: (Name), my name is (Name).

Robbie: Oh I'm sorry, (Name), I don't know what's gotten into me, I'm so discombobulated I can hardly remember my own name.

Name: Robbie, what got you so distracted this morning?

Robbie: Well, it's just that I've got so much to do to get ready for my family reunion that I keep getting distracted.

Name: You know, Robbie, this reminds me of the gospel lesson for this morning.

Robbie: Does Jesus have a recipe for macaroni salad?

Name: No, but he does have a recipe to stay calm!

Robbie: Boy, could I use that.

Name: In this morning's gospel lesson, Jesus and his friends are invited to the house of his friend Martha and her sister Mary.

Robbie: Jesus coming? Oh my, I'd flip out! I mean, I didn't dust or have the donkey cleaned. I didn't have time to get out my best dishes, or even clean the bath...

Name: Okay, okay, we get it, Robbie! You're acting like Martha, a little overwhelmed.

Robbie: A *little* overwhelmed? Are you *kidding*? And what have *you* been doing? Just standing there talking to Jesus, blah, blah, blah. Pick up a dishcloth would you?

Name: That's just what Martha said to Jesus. She said, "Hey, Jesus, I'm glad you're here, but about Mary. Do you think you could tell her to lend a hand instead of just sitting around with you and chatting?"

Robbie: You go, Martha!

Name: But Jesus said, "I appreciate all your hospitality, Martha, but maybe you've gone a little overboard."

Robbie: Huh!

Name: Jesus said to Martha, "You know, I think maybe Mary's got the right idea. I came to visit you, but you're so distracted we haven't had a minute to be together."

Robbie: Oh I get it. Hospitality is important, but what's even more important is spending time together.

Name: I think that's it, Robbie. I know how much you're looking forward to your family reunion, but don't let all the preparations distract you from the main reason you're getting together.

Robbie: You mean it's *not* about the macaroni salad?

Name: Well, I know everyone may be looking forward to a mean macaroni salad, but what everyone is *most* looking forward to is...

Robbie: Being together...

Name: Sharing our stories...

Robbie: Sharing the love we have for one another...

Name: It's how we share God's love for us.

Robbie: Question, (Name).

Name: What's that, Robbie?

Robbie: Do you know of a caterer who does macaroni salad for 100?

Name: Amen.

Robbie: Amen.

Proper 12 [17]

Sunday between July 24 and July 30 inclusive

Luke 11:1–13

11:1 He was praying in a certain place, and after he had finished, one of his disciples said to him, "Lord, teach us to pray, as John taught his disciples."

11:2 He said to them, "When you pray, say: Father, hallowed be your name. Your kingdom come.

11:3 Give us each day our daily bread."

Name: Good morning, everyone! It's good to be here this morning. I wonder how Robbie's week was? Let's call him and find out. 1, 2, 3.... *Robbie!*

Robbie: Knock, knock.

Name: Who's there?

Robbie: Bread.

Name: Bread, who?

Robbie: Bread you wish I had a better joke!

Name: Oh, Robbie, that was *bad!*

Robbie: Well, it kind of reminded me of the gospel lesson for this morning.

Name: Really, Robbie?

Robbie: Really. It kind of sounds like a bad joke. Jesus tells his disciple knock and you will be let in. Ask and you'll be given what you ask for. Do you see a pony in church?

Name: No, Robbie.

Robbie: I rest my case. I prayed for a pony and...

Name: No pony! I see why you think the gospel lesson is like a bad joke; you thought Jesus said whatever you pray for, you will get.

Robbie: Exactly.

Name: But, Robbie, do you remember the prayer that Jesus taught his friends to say?

Robbie: I do, at least most of the time. Sometimes I'm like Rev. (name of minister) and I get the lines mixed up.

Name: Well, he sometimes has lots on his mind. But let's say it together. Okay?

Robbie: Okay. God, who is in heaven…

Name: Holy is your name…

Robbie: Your Kindom come….

Name: Your will be done…

Robbie: On earth…

Name: And everywhere…

Robbie: Give us today…

Name: Our daily bread – oh *now* I see where your knock-knock joke came from…

Robbie: And forgive us our mistakes?…Like bad jokes.

Name: As we forgive the jokester…

Robbie: And lead us not into temptation…

Name: But save us from temptation…

Robbie: Like praying for a pony…

Name: For your Way, God, is the Way of goodness…

Robbie: And fulfillment, forever and ever. Amen.

Robbie: So what you're saying is that Jesus wants our prayers to be about praying for the things in our lives that we really need.

Name: Like enough food for the day,.

Robbie: And that the world becomes a loving, caring place for all.

Name: And forgiving one another, and being thankful for the times we've been forgiven.

Robbie: And for not leading us down a path that makes us envious, resentful of one another.

Name: And for showing us a way of living that makes us better people.

Robbie: Because God's way is a *good* way.

Name: Now…

Robbie: And forever and ever.

Name: Amen. Robbie?

Robbie: Yes.

Name: Knock, knock.

Robbie: Come on in, I've been waiting for you to call.

Name: Amen.

Proper 13 [18]

Sunday between July 31 and August 6 inclusive

Luke 12:13–21

12:13 Someone in the crowd said to him, "Teacher, tell my brother to divide the family inheritance with me."

12:14 But he said to him, "Friend, who set me to be a judge or arbitrator over you?"

12:15 And he said to them, "Take care! Be on your guard against all kinds of greed; for one's life does not consist in the abundance of possessions."

Name: Good morning, everyone. It's good to be here this morning. I wonder how Robbie has been this week. Let's call him and find out. 1, 2, 3… *Robbie!*

Robbie: I'm rich, I'm rich, I'm rich!

Name: What?

Robbie: I said I'm rich.

Name: I heard that part, Robbie. How did you get so rich?

Robbie: Well, (Name), I was rummaging around this past week clearing out some old files in Rev. (minister's) desk, when what do I notice? The bottom drawer had a secret compartment!

Name: Oh, Robbie, I *love* secret compartments. What did you find? The deed to a magnificent castle?

Robbie: No, (Name), not that. Something much more *valuable…*

Name: Did you find the deed to a valuable lakefront property next to some celebrities so you can be invited to all the fancy parties?

Robbie: No, (Name), much better than that…

Name: Did you find the secret to how you get the caramel into the centre of those Caramilk…

Robbie: Get serious, (Name)! That's one of those great unsolvable mysteries of the universe!

Name: Sorry, Robbie. What did you find then?

Robbie: (quietly) *A map.*

Name: (loudly) A map!

Robbie: *Shhh.* Keep your voice down; do you want everyone to hear?

Name: Well that's kind of the point isn't it, Robbie?

Robbie: You're right! You know me, I can't keep good news to myself. *Yes* I found a map, but not just *any* map; it's an ancient *treasure* map.

Name: Wow, Robbie! Where did the map lead you?

Robbie: X marks the spot and the X led me right *here*.

Name: No!

Robbie: Yes! Right here and when I opened the box I found a note. It was in code: Lk 121321.

Name: Robbie, that's the gospel lesson for this morning: Luke chapter 12, verses 13 to 21. It's the story about a man who got a big inheritance. In fact it was *so* big, he didn't have enough room for it, so he spent all of his time worrying about where he was going to keep it. Eventually, he decided to build bigger storehouses for all his stuff, but there was only one problem.

Robbie: What was that?

Name: Well, Robbie, there are *two* kinds of rich. There's rich in *money*...

Robbie: Which is what the guy in the gospel was...

Name: And there's rich in love...

Robbie: What are you talking about?

Name: Well, Robbie, Jesus told the story of the rich man and his inheritance so that we'd seek the kind of treasure that lasts forever.

Robbie: God's treasure chest of love for us... .

Name: And the love we share with one another.

Robbie: So, (Name), X really does mark the spot. X is the symbol for Christ. We are marked with the cross when we're baptized. We are loved by God and that makes us...

Name: Rich.

Robbie: Rich beyond our wildest dreams!

Name: Amen, Robbie. Have a good holiday.

Robbie: You too!

Proper 14 [19]

Sunday between August 7 and August 13 inclusive

Luke 12:32–40

12:32 "Do not be afraid, little flock, for it is your Father's good pleasure to give you the kingdom.

12:33 Sell your possessions, and give alms. Make purses for yourselves that do not wear out, an unfailing treasure in heaven, where no thief comes near and no moth destroys.

12:34 For where your treasure is, there your heart will be also."

Name: Good morning, everyone! Can you believe it's August already! Time flies when you're having fun. And I'm sure Robbie's been having fun. Let's see if he can have fun with us this morning. 1, 2, 3... *Robbie!*

Name: Good morning, Robbie.

Robbie: X marks the spot!

Name: What spot?

Robbie: The spot where the treasure's at!

Name: Robbie, have you been treasure hunting on your summer holidays?

Robbie: I sure have been. I've found all kinds of treasures: cool stones, bottle caps... I even found a loonie on the ground.

Name: That's great, Robbie, because treasure is what Jesus is talking about this morning in the gospel lesson.

Robbie: Cool! When do we start our treasure hunt?

Name: We can start right now, Robbie.

Robbie: Excellent! What should we do first?

Name: Well, Jesus tells us that we can start by selling or giving away our possessions.

Robbie: (Pause) Seriously?

Name: Seriously! And the next step on our treasure hunt is to share what we have with those who are in need.

Robbie: Seriously?

Name: Seriously.

Robbie: Excuse me for being a little impatient, but when do we get to the treasure part of the gospel reading?

Name: Soon.

Robbie: Cross your heart?

Name: That's just what Jesus did!

Robbie: He did?

Name: Yes, in the gospel lesson Jesus said, "For where your treasure is, there your heart will be also."

Robbie: So Jesus' treasure was in his heart?

Name: It sure was, Robbie; his treasure was found in caring for others.

Robbie: That's good treasure!

Name: His treasure was found in inviting all people to join in God's Kindom!

Robbie: Jackpot!

Name: His treasure was in healing and helping people!

Robbie: Double jackpot!

Name: His treasure was giving his whole heart, his whole self, to the world!

Robbie: X marks the spot!

Name: And the X is in each of our hearts when we care and live for one another.

Robbie: Amen.

Proper 15 [20]

Sunday between August 14 and August 20 inclusive

Luke 12:49–56, MSG

12:49–51 "I've come to start a fire on this earth – how I wish it were blazing right now! I've come to change everything, turn everything right-side up – how I long for it to be finished! Do you think I came to smooth things over and make everything nice? Not so. I've come to disrupt and confront!"

Name: Good morning, everyone! Well change is in the air this morning. Two more Sundays and we'll be into September. I wonder how Robbie feels about summer ending? Let's ask him. 1, 2, 3… *Robbie!*

Name: Good morning, Robbie!

Robbie: Fire!

Name: Well I know the church can be awfully hot in the summer, but I think you're exaggerating a bit.

Robbie: No, "fire" is what Jesus was telling the world this morning.

Name: Oh, Robbie, you're talking about the gospel lesson this morning.

Robbie: I sure hope our fire insurance is up to date.

Name: Robbie…

Robbie: Are the smoke alarms working?

Name: Robbie…

Robbie: Hey, there's no fire extinguisher in the castle! (Name), is this castle up to code?

Name: I'll bring it up with the property committee. But you know, Robbie, I think you're right; Jesus was certainly on fire!

Robbie: But in a good way, like when I get excited I can't help but breathe a little fire myself!

Name: Jesus was on fire telling people that God's love wasn't just for *some* people.

Robbie: But for *everyone!*

Name: Jesus was on fire telling people that God's justice was coming not just for *some.*

Robbie: But for *everyone!*

Name: He was all fired up telling people that the church was going to be welcoming not just for *some.*

Robbie: But for *everyone!*

Name: This change was going to be like a huge fire clearing out the "dead wood."

Robbie: And making room for the new growth of God's way!

Name: Are you ready?

Robbie: I'm ready! Let's keep the fire of God's love.

Name: And God's justice.

Robbie: Burning in our hearts and lives.

Name: Amen.

Proper 16 [21]

Sunday between August 21 and August 27

Jeremiah 1:4–10, MSG

1:4 Now the word of the Lord came to me saying,

1:5 "Before I formed you in the womb I knew you, and before you were born I consecrated you; I appointed you a prophet to the nations."

1:6 Then I said, "Ah, Lord God! Truly I do not know how to speak, for I am only a boy."

Name: Good morning, everyone! Well, can you believe it? Today is the last Sunday of August! Soon kids will be saying goodbye to the summer and getting ready to go back to school. I wonder what Robbie's got to say about that? Let's call him. 1, 2, 3... *Robbie!*

Name: Good morning, Robbie!

Robbie: I don't know what to say.

Name: That's not like you, Robbie, you usually have lots to say.

Robbie: "I don't know what to say!" That's what Jeremiah said.

Name: Oh, you're talking about the lesson for this morning.

Robbie: Exactly! God told Jeremiah to speak to the nations! I get nervous just speaking to you, (Name). I can't imagine how nervous Jeremiah was when he was told to speak to the world!

Name: You know, Robbie, I think we all get nervous when we have to speak up for God's way. I get nervous too!

Robbie: Not you, (Name), you're always so poised and confident!

Name: Not always, Robbie. Sometimes I'm nervous to share how God is in my life.

Robbie: Why are you nervous to talk about God?

Name: Well, Robbie, sometimes I get nervous because I'm afraid people will think I'm weird.

Robbie: Uhhh, (Name)? We already know you're weird, but no more weird than the rest of us!

Name: Well, uh, thanks, Robbie.

Robbie: When you talk about God, it doesn't sound weird at all.

Name: Really?

Robbie: You talk about how God loves us.

Name: That's not weird?

Robbie: Not at all. You talk about how God created us to love one another.

Name: That doesn't sound too weird.

Robbie: It's not. It's great! You talk about how we should be caring to those that others find difficult.

Name: That's hard to do sometimes but it doesn't sound too weird?

Robbie: And you talk about how we should care for the earth just like God cares for us.

Name: That sounds good.

Robbie: It *is* good! See you're just like Jeremiah.

Name: He thought he didn't know what to say about God's way.

Robbie: But God gave him the words.

Name: And the courage.

Robbie: To speak!

Name: Maybe I could try speaking with a Scottish accent.

Robbie: Now that would be weird!

Name: Amen.

Robbie: Amen.

Proper 17 [22]

Sunday between August 28 and September 3 inclusive

Luke 14:1, 7–14

14:1 On one occasion when Jesus was going to the house of a leader of the Pharisees to eat a meal on the Sabbath, they were watching him closely.

14:7 When he noticed how the guests chose the places of honor, he told them a parable.

Name: Good morning, everyone. It's a great day to be together! But someone's missing. Do you know who it is? That's right, Robbie. Let's call him and see if he's home. 1, 2, 3... *Robbie!*

Name: Good morning, Robbie. How are you this morning?

Robbie: Not so great.

Name: I'm sorry to hear that, Robbie. What's the matter?

Robbie: My tummy hurts.

Name: Oh no. Was it something you ate?

Robbie: I don't think so

Name: Do you have a fever? (checks Robbie's forehead)

Robbie: I don't think so.

Name: Hmmm. When did your tummy start hurting?

Robbie: It started hurting at school on Friday during recess.

Name: Did you get hurt while playing?

Robbie: I think that's the problem. I wasn't playing.

Name: Why not?

Robbie: I wasn't chosen!

Name: You weren't chosen?

Robbie: We were going to play dragon touch football. Ten dragons on each team but...

Name: But?

Robbie: But there were 21 dragons. And I didn't get picked.

Name: I'm so sorry, Robbie. That must have felt awful?

Robbie: It sure did. It felt so bad my tummy started to hurt!

Name: You know, Robbie, your story reminds me of the gospel lesson for this morning.

Robbie: We're not picking teams for dragon football I hope?

Name: No, Robbie, this morning Jesus is talking about being included as part of God's team.

Robbie: Is it a big team?

Name: Massive.

Robbie: Do we get to wear a cool jersey?

Name: No special jersey.

Robbie: Do we need special equipment?

Name: You're already fully equipped.

Robbie: I am?

Name: Yes, you are. Do you know how to welcome people when they are new?

Robbie: Sure, I smile, say hello, ask them their name and introduce them to other people I know.

Name: See you're already a great member of God's team.

Robbie: What else do I need to do to be on God's team?

Name: Well, on God's team the rules are Number 1: Look out for others.

Robbie: If someone's sad.

Name: Be a comfort.

Robbie: If someone's left out.

Name: Invite them in.

Robbie: If someone's hurt.

Name: Try to make them feel better.

Robbie: You know what, (Name)?

Name: What's that, Robbie?

Robbie: I like being on God's team.

Name: Me too! How's the tummy?

Robbie: Much better, thanks to your care.

Name: Amen.

Proper 18 [23]

September 4 to September 10 inclusive

Luke 14:25–33, MSG

14:25–27 One day when large groups of people were walking along with him, Jesus turned and told them, "Anyone who comes to me but refuses to let go of father, mother, spouse, children, brothers, sisters – yes, even one's own self! – can't be my disciple. Anyone who won't shoulder his own cross and follow behind me can't be my disciple.

14:33 "Simply put, if you're not willing to take what is dearest to you, whether plans or people, and kiss it good-bye, you can't be my disciple."

Name: Good morning, everyone! I've sure missed Robbie. I hope he's had a good summer and a good first week of school. Let's call him. 1, 2, 3... *Robbie!*

Name: Good morning, Robbie!

Robbie: Whatever.

Name: Robbie, that doesn't sound like you. What do you *mean* whatever?

Robbie: I'm sorry, I just having a bit of a hard time adjusting.

Name: Adjusting to what?

Robbie: The change.

Name: The change?

Robbie: Yes, up until Monday everything was great. I'd sleep in the mornings; I didn't worry about what I was going to wear…

Name: Robbie, don't you wear the same outfit every day?

Robbie: That's not the point. In the summer I'd jump out of bed when I felt like it, I'd stay up late; I'd play with my friends all day long, and then…*bam.*

Name: Oh I think I understand, Robbie; you're having a hard time letting go of summer and moving into the fall.

Robbie: That's for sure.

Name: You know, Robbie, it kind of reminds me of Jesus.

Robbie: Really? Did Jesus have a bedtime; did Jesus have to make sure he packed a lunch for the next day? Did Jesus have homework instead of playing with his friends?

Name: I don't know, Robbie, but Jesus *did* have to let go of things.

Robbie: Like what.

Name: Well, he had to let go of his mom and his dad when he set out to teach the world about God's love.

Robbie: And?

Name: And he had to let go of his hometown so he could go and teach to the world about God's forgiveness, and teach us to forgive one another.

Robbie: And?

Name: He had to let go of his mother's cooking.

Robbie: That's not so bad; I heard his mom wasn't a great cook.

Name: Robbie!

Robbie: Well it's true.

Name: The point is, Robbie, can you imagine what would have happened if Jesus just said, "I'm not letting go of my home, I'm too scared to leave my friends, I'm not letting go"?

Robbie: I guess we wouldn't be here now would we.

Name: That's right, Robbie. If Jesus wasn't willing to let go of some things, we never would have heard of him, and…

Robbie: And we never would have learned about God's hope for us – for justice, for kindness, for loving our neighbour.

Name: That's right.

Robbie: But letting go is so…*uncomfortable*.

Name: That's true, Robbie. Change can be uncomfortable. Letting go can be hard to do, but when we let go it can make room for other things in our life and in the lives of others.

Robbie: I see your point. Letting go of summer means saying hello to fall; it may mean making new friends.

Name: Letting go can make room for us to share God's love with others.

Robbie: Letting go can set us free to be the loving, caring, sharing people God hopes we will become.

Name: Amen.

Proper 19 [24]

Sunday between September 11 and September 17 inclusive

Luke 15:1–10, MSG

15:4–7 "Suppose one of you had a hundred sheep and lost one. Wouldn't you leave the ninety-nine in the wilderness and go after the lost one until you found it? When found, you can be sure you would put it across your shoulders, rejoicing, and when you got home call in your friends and neighbors, saying, 'Celebrate with me! I've found my lost sheep!' Count on it – there's more joy in heaven over one sinner's rescued life than over ninety-nine good people in no need of rescue."

Name: Good morning, everyone. I'm sure glad to be here this morning and I'm really looking forward to seeing Robbie. Let's call him. 1, 2, 3... *Robbie!*

Robbie: (wearing a lamb's head) Baaa!

Name: Robbie, is that you?

Robbie: Baaa!

Name: Robbie!

Robbie: Oh (Name), you saw right through my disguise.

Name: Why are you trying to disguise yourself?

Robbie: Well, it's because I'm feeling a little bit sheepish this morning.

Name: Sheepish?

Robbie: Yeah, I'm feeling a little bit ashamed.

Name: Why are you feeling ashamed, Robbie?

Robbie: Well, it all started last week after the service. I was supposed to help clean up the castle.

Name: I remember, Robbie. You and I decided that the castle needed some tidying up so we made a plan to stay after the service to take care of business.

Robbie: Only...

Name: Only after the service I looked all over for you but you were nowhere to be found.

Robbie: I was a "BAAA-D" dragon. You see, friends of mine came by and asked me to go to the park with them and I sort of forgot to stay and help clean.

Name: You *sort of* forgot?

Robbie: Well, not really, (Name). I sort of chose to go with my friends rather than stay and help clean up.

Name: I see.

Robbie: I'm really sorry, (Name), I've felt bad all week and I didn't know if you'd welcome me back this morning?

Name: You know, Robbie, this reminds me of the gospel lesson this morning.

Robbie: Really?

Name: Really. In the gospel lesson, Jesus tells us about a sheep that lost its way.

Robbie: Directionally challenged?

Name: Sort of. You know sheep usually follow their shepherd.

Robbie: True. But you know, (Name), sheep are easily distracted.

Name: And when they are distracted they sometimes forget to follow the shepherd.

Robbie: And that's when they can get into trouble.

Name: True enough. But Jesus tells us that a good shepherd doesn't just forget about the sheep that has lost its way. Even though the shepherd has lots of sheep, each sheep is precious. So the shepherd keeps looking, hoping to find the sheep.

Robbie: When the shepherd finds the lost lamb, doesn't she get mad at the lamb for getting lost in the first place?

Name: The gospel tells us that even though the lamb got lost the shepherd is *so* happy that the lamb is found that she picks him up and gives him a big hug because she loves the lamb so much.

Robbie: (Name), I'm sorry I didn't stay and help clean up the castle.

Name: I know you are, Robbie. I'm just so glad that you found your way back to (church name).

Robbie: And I'm so glad you kept looking for me.

Name: You know, Robbie, we all lose our way sometimes, but the good news is that God continues to call us back to be part of the family.

Robbie: By the way, the castle looks great except I think you missed a spot.

Name: Robbie!

Robbie: I mean it's *perfect*. Amen.

Name: Amen.

Proper 20 [25]

Sunday between September 18 and September 24 inclusive

Jeremiah 8:18 – 9:1

8:18 My joy is gone, grief is upon me, my heart is sick.

8:20 "The harvest is past, the summer is ended, and we are not saved."

8:21 For the hurt of my poor people I am hurt, I mourn, and dismay has taken hold of me.

8:22 Is there no balm in Gilead?

Name: Good morning, everyone! Wow, I can't believe September is almost over. Pretty soon we'll be pulling out our mittens and winter coats! I wonder how Robbie is this fine morning. Let's call him.
1, 2, 3… *Robbie!*

Name: Good morning, Robbie.

Robbie: (replies sadly) Mornin'.

Name: Why so glum, chum?

Robbie: I can't believe summer is really *over!* No more lazy days of sunshine. Now I have to wear a coat when I go outside, the water in my moat is too cold to swim in…I feel like Jeremiah!

Name: Jeremiah?

Robbie: From the reading this morning: Jeremiah say's "My joy is gone! My heart is sick!" The harvest is past, the summer is ended.

Name: Wow, Robbie, you really *are* bummed out.

Robbie: I sure am.

Name: I wonder, Robbie, is there no balm that can sooth you?

Robbie: Wait a minute, (Name), I'm a little down, but you don't need to blow me up!

Name: Blow you up?

Robbie: You said "bomb." Bombs blow things up.

Name: No, no, Robbie. There are bombs that blow things up and you spell that kind of bomb B O M B. But there is another kind of balm, a balm that soothes, and you spell that one B A L M.

Robbie: And you're talking about the balm that soothes?

Name: Just like Jeremiah did. When things were difficult for his people, Jeremiah asked God if there was any balm that could make them feel better?

Robbie: And was there?

Name: Well, Robbie, I think God told Jeremiah that *he* was the balm.

Robbie: Not the blow-up kind but the healing kind.

Name: Right. God told Jeremiah he was supposed to be a balm of healing for the nation.

Robbie: Jeremiah was a balm of hope to people who were feeling hopeless.

Name: Jeremiah was a balm of courage, when he spoke up for the people who were being hurt by others.

Robbie: Jeremiah was the balm of God when he taught people that following God's way was healing. You know, (Name), you're kinda the balm yourself!

Name: How so?

Robbie: I was feeling down and grumpy, but you still listen to me; you care for me; you love me.

Name: Well I'm glad I can be the balm for you, Robbie, and you know what?

Robbie: What's that?

Name: You're the balm for me and (church name) too!

Robbie: I guess God calls us to be the balm to one another.

Name: Amen.

Robbie: Kaboom!

Proper 21 [26]

Sunday between September 25 and October 1 inclusive

Luke 16:19–31

16:19 "There was a rich man who was dressed in purple and fine linen and who feasted sumptuously every day.

16:20 And at his gate lay a poor man named Lazarus, covered with sores…"

Name: Good morning, everyone! It's great to be here today. I wonder if Robbie is home? Let's call him. 1, 2, 3… *Robbie!*

Robbie: (singing) Wasted days and wasted nights!

Name: Robbie, what are you doing?

Robbie: Practicing.

Name: Practicing what?

Robbie: My gospel song.

Name: Your gospel song?

Robbie: Yeah, the gospel says a man wasted his life, he spent his life getting stuff, and he spent his time thinking about how to get more stuff.

Name: Oh I see, Robbie. You're talking about the story about a rich man who thought a good life was about shopping and getting. That those things would make him complete.

Robbie: That's right. Richie Rich was so in love with stuff and with the idea of getting *more* stuff, he couldn't see anything else.

Name: And then there is Lazarus. The rich man sure didn't see poor Lazarus. Lazarus, who didn't have two pennies to rub together. Lazarus, whose only friends were the neighbourhood dogs who would come and lick his wounds.

The story goes, that when Lazarus died, he was taken up by angels and placed in the arms of Abraham.

Robbie: Abraham was a good man.

Name: He was the father of Israel, of all the Jewish people. So if Lazarus, the poorest man is united with Abraham, that was a sign of God's compassion and love for the weakest and the poorest. But the rich man…

Robbie: Burn, baby, burn!

Name: Robbie, you have to remember this is just a story; Lazarus and the rich man were not *real* people.

Robbie: Okay, okay. But the rich man, when he died, he asks for mercy, just a drop of water, to cool him.

Name: But Abraham says…

Robbie: (singing) "It's too late, baby now, it's just too late."

Name: Kind of. Abraham says, "Rich man, I gave you lots of chances to have a good life – a life to seek love and justice with your neighbours, a life to share what you have with others, a life to be full of compassion for others and for yourself, but you chose to spend your life getting stuff and spent all your time thinking about how to get *more* stuff."

Robbie: And the rich man realized that he had spent his life pursuing stuff that doesn't last.

Name: And, when he realized this, he wanted to tell all his brothers and sisters not to do what he had done in his life. So he asked Abraham to send an angel to them to tell them what makes for a full and good life.

Robbie: But Abraham said, "Hey, I already did that. I've sent lots of people to tell you the way to a purposeful and meaningful life. There was Moses and all the prophets, for instance, but you wouldn't listen to them. I don't think even an angel could help change their hearts."

Name: The end. So the moral of this story is…

Robbie: You snooze, you lose.

Name: Kind of. Jesus told this story because he wanted people to wake up before it was too late. He wanted them to wake up to being kind, to seeking justice for all people, to realize that the best things in life are love that is shared and our relationships with one another.

Robbie: Like I said, he didn't want people waking up one day and the only song they know is "Wasted days and wasted nights."

Name: Amen.

Proper 22 [27]

Sunday between October 2 and October 8 inclusive

Luke 17:5–10, MSG

17:5 The apostles came up and said to the Master, "Give us more faith."

17:6 But the Master said, "You don't need *more* faith. There is no 'more' or 'less' in faith. If you have a bare kernel of faith, say the size of a poppy seed, you could say to this sycamore tree, 'Go jump in the lake,' and it would do it."

Name: Good morning, everyone! It's wonderful to see everyone here this morning. I wonder how Robbie's week was? Let's call him and find out. 1, 2, 3...*Robbie!*

Name: Good morning, Robbie, how are you?

Robbie: Not bad, more or less.

Name: What do you mean, *more or less?*

Robbie: I'm talking about the gospel lesson this morning.

Name: Oh, right. In the lesson this morning, Jesus' friends ask him to give them more faith. Is that right?

Robbie: More or less.

Name: But Jesus says to them, "You don't need more faith. There is no more or less in faith." Is that right?

Robbie: More or less.

Name: Jesus was telling his friends that they had all the faith they needed to follow God's way.

Robbie: A little dab will do you.

Name: Sometimes less is more.

Robbie: Like if I'm having a bad day and someone gives me a hug. I can feel better. A hug can be a small thing, but it can make a big change.

Name: Small things count.

Robbie: Or when someone forgets their lunch and I share mine with them, even if it's just a little.

Name: A little can go a long way!

Robbie: Or if I see someone crying and I ask them if they are okay.

Name: Just that small act of caring can go a long way to making someone feel better.

Robbie: So we've got tons of faith potential inside each one of us.

Name: And all those little faith acts add up for a gigantic boost in faith.

Robbie: More or less!

Name: Maybe that's exactly what Jesus was telling his friends; faith is often found in the small things. Bigger doesn't mean better in God's Kindom.

Robbie: That's good to know. I was worried I didn't have enough faith.

Name: No need to worry, Robbie, your faith always gives us a lift. Get it? Faith lift?

Robbie: Got it. Amen.

Proper 23 [28]

Sunday between October 9 and October 15 inclusive

Luke 17:11–19

17:11 On the way to Jerusalem, Jesus was going through the region between Samaria and Galilee.

17:12 As he entered a village, ten lepers approached him. Keeping their distance,

17:13 they called out, saying, "Jesus, Master, have mercy on us!" When he saw them, he said to them, "Go and show yourselves to the priests." And as they went, they were made clean.

Name: Happy thanksgiving, everyone! I sure am thankful to be with everyone this morning. I'm hoping that Robbie can join our thanksgiving service. Let's call him. 1, 2, 3… *Robbie!*

Robbie: Thanks a lot!

Name: Why do you say that, Robbie?

Robbie: Because I've got a lot to be thankful for.

Name: Me, too, which is why I can't understand it.

Robbie: Understand what?

Name: The guys in the gospel lesson this morning.

Robbie: Oh, you mean the people who were sick and went to Jesus for healing.

Name: Yeah, they were *really* sick. Back in Jesus' day, leprosy was a disease that couldn't be cured. Nobody wanted to be around people with that sickness. It was terminal.

Robbie: Like the airport.

Name: No, Robbie, not *that* kind of terminal. Terminal means you eventually die from the sickness.

Robbie: It must have been terrible to be terminal.

Name: Which is why I don't understand why only one out of the ten men that Jesus helped returned to say thank you.

Robbie: Well, I've been looking at rates of return and 10% seems pretty good these days.

Name: I guess you're right, Robbie. Jesus didn't count the cost. He just healed and helped people because he hoped it would help and heal the world.

Robbie: You know, (Name), sometimes I forget to be thankful. Sometimes I get so excited about something that I forget to say thanks.

Name: Me too, Robbie. But when I remember that I forgot to say or give thanks, I can say thank you even later.

Robbie: Maybe that's what happened to the other nine guys. I like to think that in the excitement of being helped they forgot to give thanks.

Name: But maybe later they remembered and said thank you.

Robbie: To Jesus.

Name: To God.

Robbie: Or maybe they passed on the healing to others who needed it. Thanks, (Name).

Name: Thank *you*, Robbie. Amen.

Proper 24 [29]

Sunday between October 16 and October 22 inclusive

Luke 18:1–8

18:2 He said, "In a certain city there was a judge who neither feared God nor had respect for people.

18:3 In that city there was a widow who kept coming to him and saying, 'Grant me justice against my opponent.'"

Name: Good morning, everyone! It's good to see you this morning. You know, Robbie told me this week that it does his heart *so* much good to see you on Sunday morning that he feels good for the rest of the week. Let's see if Robbie is home this week. On the count of three: 1, 2, 3… *Robbie!*

Robbie: (Doesn't come out of castle)

Name: Hmmm, I wonder what the problem is? Let's try it again and see if we can't wake Robbie up. 1, 2, 3… *Robbie!*

Robbie: (Nothing)

Name: Wow, this is harder than I thought. What do you think we should do? Do you think we should give up and go home? (Ask the kids.) Well, I think we should try again. Are you with me? Okay. *1, 2, 3…Robbie!*

Robbie: (Robbie comes out) Good morning, (Name), morning everyone. Boy, I was trying to sleep in today, I heard you call me once, and I turned over on my pillow! I heard you call me twice and I put the pillow over my head. I heard you call me three times and it was no use. I thought I might as well get up because I won't get any rest this morning. Sometimes, (Name), you're just like an old woman!

Name: Excuse me, Robbie!

Robbie: That's right, just like the old woman in the Bible reading today.

Name: Oh, you mean the old woman that went to see the judge so that she would get treated fairly?

Robbie: Of course that's what I mean, (Name), what did you think? That I was calling you names? The woman in the Bible lesson today was old and she didn't have anyone to take care of her. In fact, she had been cheated out of her house and money. So she went to the judge because she wanted to be treated fairly!

Name: And the judge treated her fairly!

Robbie: Not at first, (Name). At first the judge didn't want to listen to the widow, he'd just say, "Case denied. Next case," and she'd be escorted away.

Name: Oh that's sad, Robbie.

Robbie: Well, (Name), it *would* be if that were the end of the story, but it's not. No. That old widow woman was *feisty!* Like great old ladies can get! She didn't give up, (Name), no sir! She was back in front of the judge every day. I imagine she even went to his house and stood outside his door calling for justice.

Name: That *would* be annoying!

Robbie: I imagine when he was having lunch with his friends, she would show up at his table and ask for justice.

Name: How embarrassing!

Robbie: It got to the point where the judge was always looking over his shoulder, afraid the old widow lady would appear. He could hardly sleep at night. I'm sure she'd even go into the men's room where she wasn't supposed to be to plead her case!

Name: Oh my gosh, that woman would not give up!

Robbie: No she wouldn't. In fact, she was driving the judge bananas. So finally the judge said to the woman.

Name: "Though I have no fear of God and no respect for anyone, yet because this widow keeps bothering me, I will grant her justice, so that she may not wear me out by continually coming."

Robbie: So her persistence paid off!

Name: It sure did and you know, Robbie, Jesus told his friends this story because he said we should be that persistent in praying and caring for one another and for the earth. Even if we don't see results or get what we want right away, keep at it! God's love and justice will come!

Robbie: (Name)?

Name: Yes?

Robbie: Can I have a puppy?

Name: No, Robbie, you can't.

Robbie: Can I have a puppy?

Name: I'll think about it.

Robbie: (Name)? Can I have a puppy?

Name: Goodbye, Robbie, I'll see you next week.

Robbie: You sure will, (Name)! And don't think I'll forget! I've learned a valuable lesson today.

Name: Amen, Robbie.

Proper 25 [30]

Sunday between October 23 and October 29 inclusive

Luke 18:9–14

18:9 He also told this parable to some who trusted in themselves that they were righteous and regarded others with contempt:

18:10 "Two men went up to the temple to pray, one a Pharisee and the other a tax collector."

Name: Good morning, everyone. It sure is good to be back again this week and to have a chance to talk to Robbie. Let's see if he is home. 1, 2, 3...*Robbie!*

Robbie: Good morning, (Name). (Looks sad)

Name: Why so glum, chum?

Robbie: Well, I didn't have a very good week at school.

Name: What happened, Robbie?

Robbie: Well my friends and I were having lunch together and then we started to compare our lunches; and, (Name), you know that I always have oatmeal sandwiches?

Name: I know how much you love oatmeal, Robbie.

Robbie: Well one of my friends had sushi for lunch, another one had pizza, and one even had lobster bisque!

Name: Wow, Robbie, your friends sure had different lunches.

Robbie: I know, but then the friend who had sushi said, "An oatmeal sandwich? I'm glad I'm not like you! I have such a better lunch." And then the friend who had pizza said, "I'm thankful that *I* didn't get an oatmeal sandwich; my pizza is *sooo* much better." Then the friend who had the lobster bisque said, "I think we should eat somewhere else; I wouldn't want to be seen eating with an oatmeal sandwich eater!" And they all moved to another table.

Name: That's awful, Robbie. I can understand why you were so upset. It reminds me of the gospel story this morning.

Robbie: Is there a passage on oatmeal?

Name: No, Robbie. The gospel story today is about two people. One man is a church leader. And the other man is a tax collector. Both people go the church to pray.

Robbie: I remember this story! The Pharisee thought he was really special, so when he came to church he went right to the front of the church so everyone could see him.

Name: And the other person was a tax collector and nobody wanted to sit beside *him*, so he sat way off in the corner.

Robbie: I know what that's like.

Name: Both were at the church to pray. The Pharisee's prayer was all about how good he was, how he was so much better than the tax collector, how his clothes were better, his offerings were better, his teeth were whiter, and his hair was perfect.

Robbie: Really, (Name)?

Name: Pretty much, except for maybe the hair and teeth thing. The point is that what he called a prayer was just a list of how he was better than everyone else.

Robbie: And the tax collector: his prayer was different. He *knew* he wasn't perfect. Far from it. But his prayer was that he wanted help being a better person.

Name: So which person do you think really came to pray?

Robbie: I guess they both *thought* they did. But Jesus taught us to care for one another and to love one another and to love ourselves. The church leader's prayer could really use some love and compassion for others, and maybe the tax collector could learn to love himself. But there's one thing I do know for sure.

Name: What's that, Robbie?

Robbie: Well, I think that if the Pharisee is praying about lunch, he should get a big slice of humble pie!

Name: Robbie, that's pretty much what Jesus said: "for all who exalt themselves will be humbled, but all who humble themselves will be exalted." Amen, Robbie. It's been great to see you.

Robbie: Same here, (Name). A bit of advice before you go…

Name: What's that?

Robbie: Stay clear of the lobster bisque!

Proper 26 [31]

Sunday between October 30 and November 5 inclusive

Luke 19:1–10

19:1 He entered Jericho and was passing through it.

19:2 A man was there named Zacchaeus; he was a chief tax collector and was rich.

19:3 He was trying to see who Jesus was, but on account of the crowd he could not, because he was short in stature.

19:4 So he ran ahead and climbed a sycamore tree to see him, because he was going to pass that way.

19:5 When Jesus came to the place, he looked up and said to him, "Zacchaeus, hurry and come down; for I must stay at your house today."

19:6 So he hurried down and was happy to welcome him.

19:7 All who saw it began to grumble and said, "He has gone to be the guest of one who is a sinner."

Name: Good morning, everyone! I hope everyone is good today and ready for some good trick or treats with Robbie. Let's see if we can trick him this morning. On the count of three, let's say George! 1, 2, 3… *George!*

Robbie: (Comes out and does a double take) Uh…sorry I thought you called me?

Name: Oh, Robbie, I'm sorry. We were just playing a trick or treat prank.

Robbie: Ohh. (Sarcastically) Ha, ha, good one. You know, (Name), your little trick kind of reminds me of the gospel lesson this morning.

Name: The "trick" or the "treat" part?

Robbie: Both. First, the trick. The gospel story is about Zacchaeus and Jesus. First thing you have to know is that Zacchaeus was not very tall. And because he wasn't tall, people would play tricks on him.

Name: Like taking his sandal and holding it up over their heads and making Zacchaeus jump for it?

Robbie: That's the sort of mean dirty tricks they'd play!

Name: Or like in the gospel lesson this morning: Jesus was coming to town and everyone wanted to see him! So they all crowded around Jesus but because Zacchaeus was not very tall…

Robbie: People kept pushing Zacchaeus to the back of the crowd, and he couldn't see.

Name: But Zacchaeus had a few tricks of his own. And one trick was that he was able to climb trees. On the day Jesus came, there was a tree nearby, so Zacchaeus climbed it and he could see Jesus perfectly.

Robbie: And Jesus could see Zacchaeus perfectly. Here's where the treat part comes in. Jesus said to Zacchaeus, "Hey, Zach, I see you and I want you and me to have supper together."

Name: Treat!

Robbie: Super, supper, treat!

Name: Exactly! But some of the people thought they had been tricked, because Jesus picked Zacchaeus and they didn't think Jesus should have supper with someone they thought wasn't as good as them.

Robbie: But having supper with the most unlikely character sounds exactly like something Jesus would do.

Name: Like when he said the last shall be first.

Robbie: That's pretty tricky!

Name: But it was a treat to those who are always last.

Robbie: Or blessed are those who are sad.

Name: Because Jesus said, "You will be comforted."

Robbie: Jesus is sure a tricky and treaty kind of guy.

Name: Amen to that!

Robbie: Jesus always looking out for the little guy. Amen.

Proper 27 [32]

Sunday between November 6 and November 12 inclusive

Psalm 98, MSG

98:4–8 Shout your praises to God, everybody!

Let loose and sing! Strike up the band!

Round up an orchestra to play for God,

Add on a hundred-voice choir.

Feature trumpets and big trombones,

Fill the air with praises to King God.

Let the sea and its fish give a round of applause,

With everything living on earth joining in.

Let ocean breakers call out, "Encore!"

And mountains harmonize the finale –

Name: Good morning, everyone! It's wonderful to be together this morning. I hope Robbie can join us to talk about today's psalm. Let's call him. 1, 2, 3… *Robbie!*

Robbie: (With a baton in his mouth.) And a 1 and a 2 and a 3…

Name: Uh, Robbie?

Robbie: Once more from the top: And a 1 and a 2 and a 3! Maybe my baton is busted?

Name: Robbie, what are you doing?

Robbie: I'm striking up the band. My gran loves this show called The Larry Welsh Show and Larry always starts the band by waving his baton and saying…

Name: I know, I know: "And a 1 and a 2 and a 3…"

Robbie: (Moment of silence) Wow, it doesn't work for you either! (Robbie taps the baton on the castle) Is this thing on? Maybe my baton needs a new battery?

Name: I don't think that's the problem, Robbie, but why this sudden interest in conducting?

Robbie: The psalm.

Name: Oh, the psalm! You want us to do what the psalmist says.

Robbie: That's right. The psalmist tells all the people to make a joyful noise!

Name: Sing songs of praise and thanksgiving!

Robbie: (increasingly excited) Screech out the high notes to God's goodness!

Name: Bang and crash the cymbals to God's love!

Robbie: (very excited) Fill the joint with the sounds of praise! And a 1 and a 2 and a 3! (silence) Maybe I should pick another key?

Name: I don't think that's the issue, Robbie!

Robbie: Well, how do we get people to praise God?

Name: Robbie, sometimes we praise God by playing music of praise.

Robbie: Apparently not everyone got the memo!

Name: And sometimes we praise God by just quietly appreciating the beauty of the world around us.

Robbie: And sometimes we sing our hymns with loud voices!

Name: And sometimes we sing softly.

Robbie: Sometimes we praise God with the sound of laughter!

Name: And sometimes we even praise God with our tears.

Robbie: So the psalmist is reminding us that God is the creator of all things! And we are all instruments of God's creation.

Name: That's right, Robbie. All the earth is an instrument of God's creation! The rocks, the trees, the wind, the rain, the oceans and lakes, all the creatures and us!

Robbie: Wow! That is quite the full orchestra! It's so wonderful that I want to make a joyful noise! And a 1, and a 2, and a 3 (singing) "Amen, Amen, Amen, Amen, Amen." Everybody! "Amen, Amen, Amen, Amen, Amen."

Proper 28 [33]

Sunday between November 13 and November 19 inclusive

Luke 21:5–19, MSG

Luke 19:5–6 One day people were standing around talking about the Temple, remarking how beautiful it was, the splendor of its stonework and memorial gifts. Jesus said, "All this you're admiring so much – the time is coming when every stone in that building will end up in a heap of rubble."

Name: Good morning, everyone! I'm sure looking forward to hearing what Robbie has to say about this morning's lesson. Let's call him. 1, 2, 3… *Robbie!*

Name: Good morning, Robbie!

Robbie: (frightened) Did you feel that!

Name: What?

Robbie: Aghhh! (goes back into the castle)

Name: Robbie, what's wrong?

Robbie: I'm worried!

Name: What are you worried about?

Robbie: Our structural integrity!

Name: The structural integrity of our building?

Robbie: That's right! No offence, but this place is old! It might even be older than you, (Name).

Name: I'm sure the building is solid, Robbie.

Robbie: Are you sure?

Name: I'm pretty sure.

Robbie: Safe to come out?

Name: Come and join us, Robbie; we're safe and sound.

Robbie: (comes out of castle)

Name: All right?

Robbie: A little better!

Name: Robbie, what's got you so spooked?

Robbie: The gospel lesson!

Name: The gospel lesson?

Robbie: Yes, did you not hear? Jesus and his friends were hanging out at the temple. They were looking at the solid walls, the great doors, the high ceiling! It was a marvellous structure!

Name: Yes, it certainly was.

Robbie: And then Jesus tells them not to get too attached to it because one day it's going to all come crashing down!

Name: Well I can certainly see why people hearing Jesus' words would be upset!

Robbie: No kidding! Can you imagine if Jesus said that about our church?

Name: Well, Robbie, he did.

Robbie: When?

Name: This morning.

Robbie: Where was I, in the washroom?

Name: No, Robbie, you were right here. The gospel lesson wasn't just for those people a long time ago. The gospel is also a reminder that our buildings won't last forever, but…

Robbie: But what?

Name: But Jesus us told us not to worry about when some things come to an end. Turn your attention to the things that last forever.

Robbie: Bell-bottoms?

Name: No.

Robbie: Jazzercise?

Name: No, Robbie! The things that last forever are things of the heart!

Robbie: Like the love we show one another.

Name: Like forgiving one another.

Robbie: Like the joy we share.

Name: Like the compassion we give.

Robbie: And the compassion we receive.

Name: That's why Jesus told his friends not to worry. Some things will end, but the things that really matter never end!

Robbie: Did you feel that?

Name: What?

Robbie: God's love!

Name: I do, Robbie, every time I meet with you! Amen.

Robbie: Amen.

Proper 29 [34]

Sunday between November 20 and November 26 inclusive

Reign of Christ Sunday

Name: Good morning, everyone. It's great to be here with you this morning. Let's see if Robbie is at home. 1, 2, 3... *Robbie!*

Name: Good morning, Robbie.

Robbie: Howdy, partner!

Name: Howdy?

Robbie: That's cowboy talk for "hi, friend."

Name: Okay. Howdy to you, too. How come we're talking cowboy today?

Robbie: I thought it would be obvious considering today is rein of Christ Sunday.

Name: What does cowboy talk have to do with reign of Christ?

Robbie: Well, last year I was at a dragon dude ranch. And when I was learning to ride a horse, the teacher said the most important thing was to hold on to your...

Name: Reins! Oh, Robbie. I'm afraid today is about a different kind of reign.

Robbie: I knew I should have worn rain boots!

Name: No, Robbie, another kind of reign.

Robbie: Seriously? How many kinds of reign are there?

Name: Well, Robbie, I think you've just about covered them all, except there is one more. You know how some countries have a king or a queen?

Robbie: Like the Queen of England.

Name: Exactly. When countries have a king or a queen as their leader, that's sometimes called their reign. They are in charge of caring for all the people and governing the country.

Robbie: Okay, so why do we call today Reign of Christ Sunday? Jesus wasn't a king.

Name: You're right. Jesus wasn't a king in the usual way we think about kings or queens, but he did talk about the Kingdom of God.

Robbie: That's true. The Kingdom of God is a kingdom where justice rules, where all people live out love.

Name: The Kingdom of God includes and cares for everyone, especially those who are left out. Like the poor, the sick, the oppressed, the vulnerable.

Robbie: That sounds like an amazing kingdom!

Name: It sure would be, Robbie. Do you know who we look to as an example of God's Kingdom?

Robbie: Uh, I'm going to go out on a limb here…is it God?

Name: Right on, Robbie, and how do we know about God?

Robbie: Uh, I could be wrong, but I'm going to say… Jesus.

Name: Right again, Robbie. As Christians, Jesus is the one who shows us God's way and God's hope for a world where justice, peace, compassion, inclusion, hope, and love rule! We call this the reign of Christ.

Robbie: So I guess I'll need to cancel the chuckwagon and the square dancing.

Name: That might be a good idea. But there is something we *can* do.

Robbie: What's that?

Name: We can round up everyone into God's corral of love and care.

Robbie: Ye ha!

Name: Amen.

Special Sundays

Thanksgiving Day

Second Monday in October (Can.)

Fourth Thursday in November (U.S.)

John 6:25–35

6:30–34 They waffled: "Why don't you give us a clue about who you are, just a hint of what's going on? When we see what's up, we'll commit ourselves. Show us what you can do. Moses fed our ancestors with bread in the desert. It says so in the Scriptures: 'He gave them bread from heaven to eat.'" Jesus responded, "The real significance of that Scripture is not that Moses gave you bread from heaven but that my Father is right now offering you bread from heaven, the *real* bread. The Bread of God came down out of heaven and is giving life to the world." They jumped at that: "Master, give us this bread, now and forever!"

Name: Good morning. It's great to be here this morning and a special welcome to all our furry guests! I'm sure Robbie is going to be excited to see you all. Should we call him? 1, 2, 3… *Robbie!*

Name: Good morning, Robbie!

Robbie: Good morning.

Name: Robbie, do you notice anything different today?

Robbie: Uh…did you get a haircut?

Name: No, Robbie.

Robbie: Are those new shoes?

Name: No, Robbie.

Robbie: Are you wearing a new cologne, something like scent de turkey?

Name: *No,* but you're getting close.

Robbie: I am? Well, give me a clue.

Name: Okay. We're celebrating a special day today.

Robbie: It can't be Halloween.

Name: No, Robbie, it's not Halloween.

Robbie: And it can't be Christmas!

Name: No, it's not Christmas,

Robbie: Easter?

Name: No.

Robbie: Groundhog Day.

Name: No

Robbie: Oh I know. It must be April Fools' day!

Name: No, Robbie.

Robbie: I give up.

Name: Well, that's kind of what the disciples were saying in the gospel lesson this morning.

Robbie: Is it Give Up Sunday?

Name: *No, Robbie!* In the gospel lesson for this morning, the disciples were trying to guess who Jesus was.

Robbie: Well, that's pretty easy. Jesus was the guy who came to share good news with the world.

Name: Good news that no matter what people tell you, you are blessed, and a beloved child of God.

Robbie: Good news was seeing your life blessed when you loved one another.

Name: Good news was caring for the children, the poor, the homeless…

Robbie: The lost and the lonely...

Name: The "least of these…"

Robbie: Even the *beasts* of these, like our four-legged friends. I'm curious, why did you ask me if I noticed anything different today?

Name: Well, Robbie, the disciples wanted Jesus to give them something that would give them more faith.

Robbie: But Jesus *did* give them something; he gave them his life, his love, his compassion, his forgiveness.

Name: Exactly, but sometimes it's hard to see that the answer is right in front of your nose. The disciples couldn't see that loving, being compassionate, being concerned about the people that others don't care for…

Robbie: These things increase your faith and bring you closer to God!

Name: Thanks for the chat, Robbie.

Robbie: I've got it!

Name: Got what?

Robbie: Got what's different about today. It's Thanksgiving Sunday! Gobble gobble.

Name: And gobble gobble to you, too! Amen.